THE BC

What chemistry, we are often asked, takes place in the succulent bosom of the sherry casks where The Macallan lies slumbering for a decade (at least) before it is allowed out to meet the bottle?

The fact is, we do not know.

It is a *matter of history*, of course, that someone in the last century discovered that whisky ages best in oaken casks which have previously contained sherry (and that today The Macallan is the *last malt whisky* exclusively to be so matured).

And it is a *matter of fact* that in goes the translucent stripling spirit. And out comes amber-gold nectar positively *billowing* with flavour.

But let us take our cue from a party of scientists whom we once invited to explore the matter. '*Magic!*' they exclaimed, swigging their drams in a most unboffinly manner. 'But magic is merely undiscovered science and we'd like to take some home *for further investigation*.'

To join our small (but devoted) band of merry malt sippers, please call 1-800-428-9810.

THE MACALLAN. THE SINGLE MALT SCOTCH.

THE MACALLAN Scotch Whisky. 43% alc./vol. Sole U.S. importer Rémy Amerique, Inc., New York, N.Y.
THE MACALLAN is a registered trademark of Macallan-Glenlivet P.L.C. © 1996 Macallan-Glenlivet P.L.C.

ELAINE

LOVES

THE PARIS REVIEW

ELAINE'S
1703 SECOND AVE
NEW YORK CITY

reservations: 534-8103/8114

The Paris Review

Founded in 1953.
Publisher Drue Heinz
Editors
George Plimpton, Peter Matthiessen, Donald Hall, Robert Silvers, Blair Fuller, Maxine Groffsky, Jeanne McCulloch, James Linville

Managing Editor	Daniel Kunitz
Editor at Large	Elizabeth Gaffney
Senior Editors	Anne Fulenwider, Brigid Hughes
Associate Editor	Stephen Clark
Assistant Editors	Ben Howe, Molly McGrann
Poetry Editor	Richard Howard
Art Editor	Joan Krawczyk
London Editor Shusha Guppy	**Paris Editor** Harry Mathews
Business Manager Lillian von Nickern	**Treasurer** Marjorie Kalman
Design Consultant	Chip Kidd

Editorial Assistants
Fiona Maazel, Quentin Rowan

Readers
Neil Azevedo, Amanda Beasley, Eliza Griswold, Sam A. Patel, Sunny Payson, Daphne Uviller

Special Consultants
Robert Phillips, Ben Sonnenberg, Remar Sutton

Advisory Editors
Nelson Aldrich, Andy Bellin, Lawrence M. Bensky, Patrick Bowles, Christopher Cerf, Jonathan Dee, Timothy Dickinson, Joan Dillon, Beth Drenning, David Evanier, Rowan Gaither, David Gimbel, Francine du Plessix Gray, Lindy Guinness, Fayette Hickox, Susannah Hunnewell, Ben Johnson, Gia Kourlas, Mary B. Lumet, Larissa MacFarquhar, Molly McKaughan, Jonathan Miller, Ron Padgett, Maggie Paley, John Phillips, Kevin Richardson, David Robbins, Philip Roth, Elissa Schappell, Frederick Seidel, Mona Simpson, Max Steele, Rose Styron, William Styron, Tim Sultan, Hallie Gay Walden, Christopher Walker, Eugene Walter, Antonio Weiss

Contributing Editors
Agha Shahid Ali, Robert Antoni, Kip Azzoni, Sara Barrett, Helen Bartlett, Robert Becker, Adam Begley, Magda Bogin, Chris Calhoun, Morgan Entrekin, Jill Fox, Walker Gaffney, Jamey Gambrell, John Glusman, Jeanine Herman, Edward Hirsch, Gerald Howard, Tom Jenks, Barbara Jones, Fran Kiernan, Joanna Laufer, Mary Maguire, Lucas Matthiessen, Dan Max, Joanie McDonnell, Christopher Merrill, David Michaelis, Dini von Mueffling, Elise Paschen, Allen Peacock, William Plummer, Charles Russell, Michael Sagalyn, David Salle, Elisabeth Sifton, Ileene Smith, Patsy Southgate, Rose Styron, William Wadsworth, Julia Myer Ward, John Zinsser

Poetry Editors
Donald Hall (1953–1961), X.J. Kennedy (1962–1964),
Thomas Clark (1964–1973), Michael Benedikt (1974–1978),
Jonathan Galassi (1978–1988), Patricia Storace (1988–1992)

Art Editors
William Pène du Bois (1953–1960), Paris Editors (1961–1974),
Alexandra Anderson (1974–1978), Richard Marshall (1978–1993)

Founding Publisher   Sadruddin Aga Khan

Former Publishers
Bernard F. Conners, Ron Dante, Deborah S. Pease

Founding Editors
Peter Matthiessen, Harold L. Humes, George Plimpton,
William Pène du Bois, Thomas H. Guinzburg, John Train

The Paris Review is published quarterly by The Paris Review, Inc. Vol. 39, No. 143, Summer 1997. Business Office: 45-39 171 Place, Flushing, New York 11358 (ISSN #0031-2037). Paris Office: Harry Mathews, 67 rue de Grenelle, Paris 75007 France. London Office: Shusha Guppy, 8 Shawfield St., London, SW3. US distributors: Random House, Inc. 1(800)733-3000. Typeset and printed in USA by Capital City Press, Montpelier, VT.   Price for single issue in USA: $10.00. $14.00 in Canada. Post-paid subscription for four issues $34.00, lifetime subscription $1000. Postal surcharge of $10.00 per four issues outside USA (excluding life subscriptions). Subscription card is bound within magazine. Please give six weeks notice of change of address using subscription card.   *While The Paris Review welcomes the submission of unsolicited manuscripts, it cannot accept responsibility for their loss or delay, or engage in related correspondence. Manuscripts will not be returned or responded to unless accompanied by self-addressed, stamped envelope.   Fiction manuscripts should be submitted to George Plimpton, poetry to Richard Howard, The Paris Review, 541 East 72nd Street, New York, N.Y. 10021.*   Charter member of the Council of Literary Magazines and Presses. This publication is made possible, in part, with public funds from the New York State Council on the Arts and the National Endowment for the Arts.   Periodicals postage paid at Flushing, New York, and at additional mailing offices.   **Postmaster:** Please send address changes to 45-39 171st Place, Flushing, N.Y. 11358.

De-stress Call

Suffering from a tension-convention? Send out an S.O.S.! Visit Hammacher Schlemmer for the relaxing "Hands-Free Massager". A massager that feels so good, once you put it on, you may never take it off.

For 147 years, Hammacher Schlemmer has consistently offered the world's greatest collection of items that are innovative, unique and just plain fun. Everything we sell is of exceptional quality and, of course, unconditionally guaranteed.

ESTABLISHED 1848

New York
147 East 57th Street
212-421-9000

Chicago
445 North Michigan Avenue
312-527-9100

Beverly Hills
309 North Rodeo Drive
310-859-7255

Acclaim for
The Reader's Catalog
A Book-of-the-Month Club Selection

"*The Reader's Catalog* is the best book without a plot."
—*Newsweek*

"The most attractively laid out and compactly informative guide that I know of to books that are currently in print."
—*The New York Times*

"A catalog of 40,000 distinguished titles, organized in 208 categories, for readers who hunger for the quality and variety available in today's mass-market bookstores. Hallelujah!"—*Time*

"A browser's paradise."
—*Library Journal*

"The scope of the endeavor is, as the kids are wont to say, awesome." —*The Baltimore Sun*

"It must be called a triumph."
—*The Los Angeles Times*

"The catalog is discriminating yet expansive, a feat of editing that anyone who has wasted time rooting out data in the weeds of the Internet will appreciate." —*Newsday*

"A valuable literary tool that's not only a reader's resource, but also a browser's delight." —*Parade Magazine*

"The best reading-group and bookstore guide available."
—*Time Out*

YOUR GUIDE TO THE 40,000 BEST BOOKS IN PRINT
THE READER'S CATALOG

TO ORDER: CALL 1-800-733-BOOK
OR VISIT YOUR LOCAL BOOKSTORE TODAY
$34.95 • Distributed by Consortium

Petaluma

1ST. AVE. AT 73RD. ST., NEW YORK CITY
772·8800

What do

Margaret Atwood, Ann Beattie, Peter Carey, Hayden Carruth, Timothy Findley, Richard Ford, Bruce Jay Friedman, Mark Leyner, Tim O'Brien, Caryl Phillips, Carol Shields, Josef Skvorecky, D.M. Thomas, and Marianne Wiggins

and many other writers have in common?

They have taught at Canada's most distinguished creative writing school, *The Humber School for Writers*.

To find out about our upcoming **summer workshop, August 2 to 8, 1997,** write to

Joe Kertes, The Humber School for Writers
Humber College, 205 Humber College Blvd.,
Toronto, Ontario, Canada M9W 5L7

or e-mail at kertes@admin.humberc.on.ca,
or call (416) 675-6622, ext. 4436, or (416) 675-5095
and leave your name and full address.

THE HUMBER SCHOOL FOR WRITERS

THE CONTEST CONSULTANT

WRITE*Time* ✓
1997

Gives you time to write!
Thousands of updates for 1997
Hundreds of New Contests

- Software designed by a writer for writers
- Lists over 2,000 contests, fellowships, scholarships, grants and awards
- Searches under categories or deadlines
- Tracks award submissions and queries
- Add or delete to create your own database

14 CATEGORIES:
Short Story
Novel
Poetry
Drama
Gay/Lesbian
Journalism
Screen/Teleplays
Residency
Nonfiction/Scholarly
Commercial
Children's Lit
Translation
Religion
Women

💾 **$80** WINDOWS/MAC

Visa/MC Accepted

1-800-891-0962
PR

WRITE*Suite*
PURCHASE BOTH FOR ONLY
💾💾 **$100**

THE MANUSCRIPT MANAGER

WRITE*Trak*

A Writer writes, WriteTrak does the rest!

WriteTrak tracks:
- SUBMISSIONS by Date, Manuscript Title, Publisher, Subject
- PUBLISHERS by Name, Submission Date, Manuscript Title
- MANUSCRIPTS by Title, Submission Date, Publisher
- EXPENSES by Date, Manuscript

UPDATES & PRINTS:
Expense Reports
Letters
Resumes
CV
Manuscripts
Publish & Submission History

💾 **$50** WINDOWS/MAC

Grossman Development Company
P.O. Box 85732, Seattle, WA 98145-1732
e-mail: gdc@earthlink.net http://www.writetime.com

SALT
SUBSCRIPTION FORM

Salt, a leading international poetry journal is published biannually. Subscribe now, and receive a FREE copy of *Salt 9*.

I would like to subscribe to *Salt*. Please send me:
❏ the next two issues for $33.95
+ postage and packaging (please specify)
within Australia ❏ $6
overseas: airmail ❏ $20
surface mail ❏ $8

❏ the next four issues for $67.80
+ postage and packaging (please specify)
within Australia ❏ $12
overseas: airmail ❏ $40
surface mail ❏ $16

❏ backlist issues, *Salt* numbers .... @$16.95 per copy
+ postage and packaging per copy (please specify)
within Australia ❏ $3
overseas: airmail ❏ $10
surface mail ❏ $4

I enclose a cheque / money order (all payments to be made in Australian dollars) or please debit my credit card (delete as applicable)
Mastercard / Bankcard / Visa

Credit Card no. _ _ _ _ / _ _ _ _ / _ _ _ _ / _ _ _ _

Expiry Date: _ _ / _ _

Name: _____

Address: _____

_____

Signature: _____ Postcode: _____

Please send to: Fremantle Arts Centre Press,
PO Box 320, South Fremantle, 6162, Australia.
Fax: (08) 9430 5242   Email: facp.iinet.net.au

BENNINGTON WRITING SEMINARS

MFA in Writing and Literature
Two-Year Low-Residency Program

**FICTION
NONFICTION
POETRY**

For more information contact:
Writing Seminars, Box PA
Bennington College
Bennington, VT 05201
802-442-5401, ext. 160
Fax 802-442-6164

FACULTY

FICTION
Douglas Bauer
Elizabeth Cox
Susan Dodd
Maria Flook
Lynn Freed
Amy Hempel
Alice Mattison
Jill McCorkle
Askold Melnyczuk

NONFICTION
Sven Birkerts
Susan Cheever
Lucy Grealy
Bob Shacochis

POETRY
April Bernard
Thomas Sayers Ellis
David Lehman
Liam Rector
Jason Shinder

POET-IN-RESIDENCE
Donald Hall

RECENT ASSOCIATE FACULTY
Robert Bly, Lucie Brock-Broido, Robert Creeley, The Dark Room Collective, Bruce Duffy, Karen Finley, Judith Grossman, Barry Hannah, Jane Hirshfield, Edward Hoagland, Lewis Hyde, Jane Kenyon, Michael Lind, Bret Lott, Carole Maso, E. Ethelbert Miller, Sue Miller, Howard Norman, Robert Pinsky, Katha Pollitt, Tree Swenson, Tom Wicker

Boston Review's *5th Annual* SHORT STORY CONTEST

Boston Review is pleased to announce its 5th Annual Short Story Contest. The winning entry will be published in the *Review*'s December 1997 issue. Stories should not exceed four thousand words and must be previously unpublished. The author's name, address, and phone should be on the first page of each entry; do not send a cover letter. A $10 processing fee, payable to *Boston Review* in the form of a check or money order, must accompany all entries. Entrants will receive a one-year subscription to the *Review* beginning with the December issue. Submissions must be postmarked by October 1, 1997. Stories will not be returned. Send entries to: Short Story Contest, *Boston Review*, E53-407 MIT, Cambridge, MA 02139.

First Prize: $1,000

92ND STREET Y
Unterberg Poetry Center

1997-98 Season of Literary Readings, Lectures & Workshops

Nadine Gordimer   William Styron   Isabel Allende   Don DeLillo

AUTHORS APPEARING THIS SEASON INCLUDE:
(in order of appearance)

W.S. Merwin ♦ Doris Lessing ♦ Richard Wilbur ♦ Margaret Drabble
Carol Shields ♦ Don DeLillo ♦ Richard Price ♦ J.M. Coetzee ♦ Amos Oz
William Styron ♦ Peter Matthiessen ♦ Jane Cooper ♦ Heather McHugh
Paul Muldoon ♦ John Guare ♦ Nadine Gordimer ♦ Ana Castillo
Elena Poniatowska ♦ Robert Wilson ♦ Frank Bidart ♦ Susan Mitchell
Alan Bennett ♦ A.R. Gurney ♦ Patrick Chamoiseau ♦ Tomás Eloy Martínez
Mary Karr ♦ Frank McCourt ♦ Isabel Allende ♦ George Steiner
Wole Soyinka ♦ Yehuda Amichai ♦ Russell Banks ♦ Gloria Naylor
Norman Mailer ♦ John Fowles

Series Membership: At $160, a Poetry Center Membership admits you to all of the above readings and much more.

SPECIAL PROGRAMS:

The Poetry of Wallace Stevens ♦ Louise Bogan at 100
An Evening of *The Odyssey*
with Robert Fagles, Jason Robards & Kathryn Walker
Chère Maître: The Flaubert-Sand Correspondence
Presented by Peter Eyre & Irene Worth
A Martin Luther King Day Tribute to Ralph Ellison
with Saul Bellow, R.W.B. Lewis, Albert Murray & others
The Making of "Ragtime" with E.L. Doctorow
Federico García Lorca at 100

Poetry Readings are co-sponsored with The Academy of American Poets.

UNTERBERG POETRY CENTER
TISCH CENTER FOR THE ARTS
1395 Lexington Ave NYC 10128
An agency of UJA-Federation

Call **996-1100**
for a brochure, which includes additional information and application guidelines, or to order tickets.

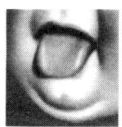 ***People say it's la crème de la crème...***
"I was immediately attracted....I could feel the restlessness of the city below the streets, hear the rumble of the subway, imagine myself back in a sunlit apartment on Bank Street or walking at night on Leroy Street with its gaslights. I recommend anyone pick up a copy..."
—*Literary Magazine Review*

"...It is exhilarating when a truly great new magazine, one which is neither transitory nor frivolous, is made available to us. Literal Latté is such a brew...it is a magazine that will surely seep into American letters and stay there." —*Small Magazine Review*

"Fresh, solidly crafted, great to read and of a high literary caliber."
—*Second Glance*

"The quality is always high." —*National Public Radio, NY & Company*

Literal Latté has published stories, poems, essays and art by
Ray Bradbury • Michael Brodsky • Robert Olen Butler
Stephen Dixon • Michael Dorris • Harlan Ellison
Allen Ginsberg • Daniel Harris • Phillip Lopate
Carole Maso • Nancy Milford • Carol Muske
Gloria Steinem • Frank Stella • John Updike • Jerry Uelsman
...and many new talents

```
┌─────────────────────────────────────────────────────────┐
│  SUBSCRIBE — $11 per year for 6 issues*                 │
│  NAME:_____  │
│  ADD:_____  │
│  PHONE:_____                          │
│  AMEX NO.:_____      EXP DATE:_____       │
│  Make checks payable to LITERAL LATTÉ 61 East 8th Street, Suite 240, │
│  NY, NY 10003 Tel: 212-260-5532 BACK ISSUES AVAILABLE — $5  │
│  *$20 for 2 years (Canada, $15 per year, International, $25 per year) │
└─────────────────────────────────────────────────────────┘
```

The Paris Review
is pleased to announce that
Karl Kirchwey
has been awarded
The Paris Review Poetic Drama Prize
for
"Alcestis: A Bedroom Comedy"
appearing in issue 142

MFA in Writing
at Vermont College

Intensive 11-day residencies on our beautiful central Vermont campus alternate with **six-month non-resident study projects.**

Residencies include classes, readings, conferences and small workshops led by two faculty. Immersed with other developing writers in a stimulating environment, students forge working relationships with each other and with experienced practitioners of poetry and fiction.

Under the careful guidance of the faculty, students focus on their own writing for the semester study project. A low student-faculty ratio (5-1) ensures close personal attention.

On-campus housing is available and residencies are catered by the award-winning New England Culinary Institute.

We also offer **a Post-Graduate Semester** and **One-Year Intensives** for those who have completed a graduate degree in creative writing.

Scholarships, minority scholarships and financial aid available

For more information please contact:
Roger Weingarten, Director
MFA in Writing, Vermont College, Montpelier, VT 05602
Tel: (802) 828-8840 Fax: (802) 828-8649

Vermont College of Norwich University

Poetry Faculty
Robin Behn
Mark Cox
Deborah Digges
Nancy Eimers
Mark Halliday
Richard Jackson
Jack Myers
William Olsen
David Rivard
J. Allyn Rosser
Mary Ruefle
Betsy Sholl
Leslie Ullman
Roger Weingarten
David Wojahn

Fiction Faculty
Carol Anshaw
Tony Ardizzone
Phyllis Barber
Francois Camoin
Abby Frucht
Douglas Glover
Sydney Lea
Diane Lefer
Ellen Lesser
Bret Lott
Sena Jeter Naslund
Christopher Noël
Pamela Painter
Sharon Sheehe Stark
Gladys Swan
W.D. Wetherell

The Paris Review

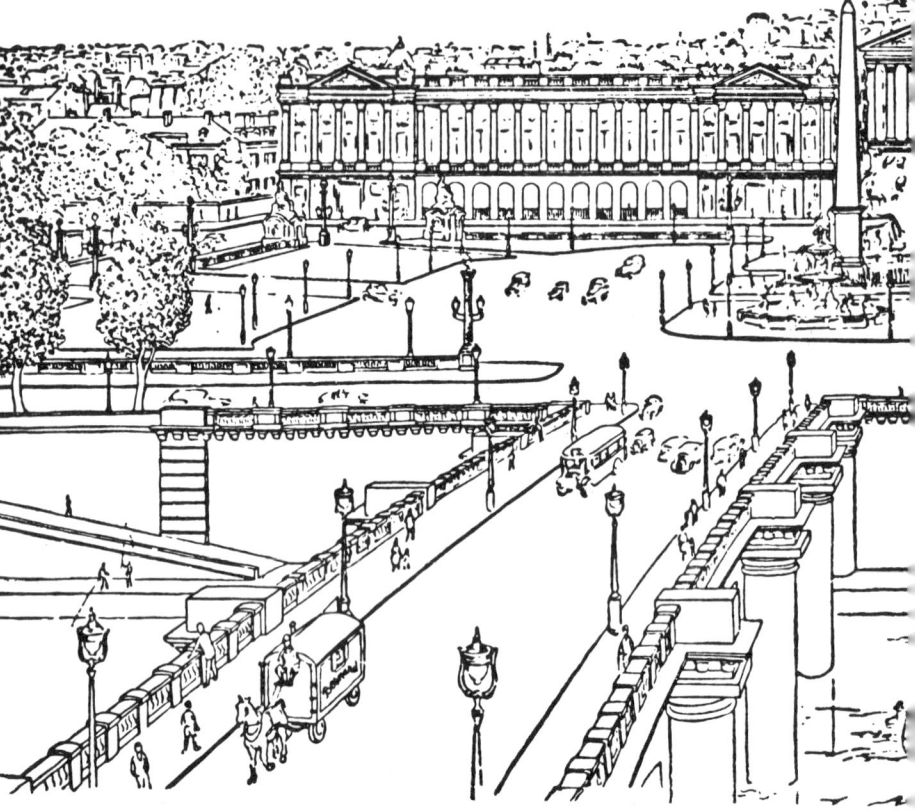

Editorial Office:
541 East 72 Street
New York, New York 10021
HTTP://www.voyagerco.com

Business & Circulation:
45-39 171 Place
Flushing, New York 11358

Distributed by Random House
201 East 50 Street
New York, N.Y. 10022
(800) 733-3000

Table of contents illustration by Billy Sullivan, ink on paper.
Frontispiece by William Pène du Bois.

Number 143

Interviews

John le Carré	*The Art of Fiction CXLIX*	50
Jan Morris	*The Art of the Essay II*	150

Fiction

David Means	*Disclaimer*	236
Joyce Carol Oates	*Ugly Girl*	114
Padgett Powell	*Aliens of Affection*	178
Charlie Smith	*Park Diary*	18

Features

Richard Brown Baker	*My Dinner with Jasper Johns*	211
Dotson Rader	*Truman Capote Meets an Idol*	103
James Salter	*Burning the Days*	75

Art

Graham Nickson	*Bathers*	107
Lynn McCarty	*Free Falling*	cover

Poetry

Claire Bateman	*Ectoplasm*	233
Bruce Bond	*Two Poems*	95
Nicholas Christopher	*Four Poems*	144
Brian Culhane	*Knowing Greek*	48
Barbara Goldberg	*Two Poems*	99
Barbara Henning	*Closure & Closure*	93
Andrew Hudgins	*Three Poems*	43
Lance Larsen	*Two Poems*	230
Rika Lesser	*536 Saratoga Avenue*	228
Sarah Lindsay	*Two Poems*	41
William Logan	*Two Poems*	39
W.S. Merwin	*Two Poems*	88
Michelangelo	*Last Poems*	91
Alan Michael Parker	*Two Poems*	226
Amanda Pecor	*Three Poems*	101
Pattiann Rogers	*The Composer, the Bone Yard*	224
Charles H. Webb	*Two Poems*	148
Rachel Wetzsteon	*Home and Away*	139

Notes on Contributors   239

Park Diary

Charlie Smith

1

There are four hundred fifty-seven names for heroin. I have learned eighty-two of them. The drug sellers tell me the names, the pushers, the smack heads, the needle-specked little boys pulling their pants down to display their swollen red puds tell me, the girls with the scratches on their arms tell me, sports at McDonald's tell me, former users tell me, a woman I met at Al-Anon, ex-junkie attending meetings because her boyfriend went back to drugs on her and beat her up, threw her down the stairs, pushed her naked into the street and left her there cowering until by chance a Universal Fellowship soup wagon came by and a (kind) soul gave her a blanket and a quarter for the phone: she tells me; and ex-hippies tell me, and a street preacher from Kansas tells me, and a cop, and a couple of social workers and a Chinese wallpaper salesman going down in flames at a party in Soma Dahlberg's penthouse tells me—*White Horse*, *Shiny*, *Doubloon*, *Red Day*, *Flash*, *Hot Jimmy*, *Alphabet Local*, *Crank*, *Pearl*, *China*

Day, Johnny, Elmo, Ajax, Yellow Blaze, are the names of heroin—*Columbus in Heaven, Deliquescence, Rainbow Roustabout, The Jeweler's Daughter, Ambivalence*, are the names of heroin—*Six Years after the Hurricane, Dead Mothers in the Highway, What is Thinkable Is Also Possible, Sweetest Love I Do Not Go For Weariness of Thee, Jumbo on Wheels*, are the names of heroin—*From This Valley They Say You Are Going Do Hasten To Bid Me Adieu But Remember The Red River Valley And The Cowboy Who Loved You So True*, are the names of heroin—and Rae tells me; like a woman speaking Japanese to the mirror, Rae tells me the names she has invented for heroin, tells me the names of her love for it, the names of what she has given up for heroin, the names of her desire and its completion, she tells me that for an addict heroin is a country with its own seasons, its own accents and inflections, its intonations and emphasis, a country of rituals and perfections, country of lonely farm lanes, and of young girls washing their hair in buckets, of children suddenly lost in a piney wood looking around; she tells me that heroin is a division of purpose and a hotel on a beach in Normandy, she puts her hand on my arm and the dry skin of her fingertips is a form of speech I have heard before, the slight erasing, shifting, whispering sound of her fingertips on my skin is the sound of a policeman weeping into his hands, and of this she tells me, of this policeman and his name which is another name for heroin, and tells me the secret mysteries of rainy nights in Nebraska where she was born, where the rain fell on the fields breaking down the green wheat—which is another name—and she tells me of the names of heroin lodged in the mouths of women dead of cholera in Bangladore, tells me the names of heroin mentioned in the abridgements of certain recent court proceedings, tells me the combined law of averages that will sweep all names of everything else that lives into the sea; Rae tells me the names and I listen, I listen to her voice that is the voice of my wife become the voice of a mad woman, and she tells me this is another of the names of heroin and I write this in my book and later say the name over to myself in case some night when my life depends on it I am asked the name and I tell them and she's freed; each of us, she tells me, naming names, is the host; each of us, she tells me, heroin calling itself *Little Mary* in her veins, is standing in the doorway, she says, like Christ just after he gets the news that everyone else in the world, but him, got crucified.

. . . smell of fish in the entranceway of the store where I buy my typing paper . . .

. . . the plane trees on the terrace beside St. Patrick's Cathedral: thick, dark green leaves, blood-fed . . .

". . . Your ass is as black as mine . . ."

Benjamin Prang says, *Accept that the world will never be healed.*

I take my earphones off, step out of the chair and sit down on the floor. Rae speaks to me, but I don't hear her. So often these days I don't hear her, or don't listen, don't want to know the latest disaster unveiled. But then I do. A mystery leaks into my ears, a noise, a sound shaping and reshaping, blips and muted screeches, whisperings and soft pleading asides, the parts of speech—fat triphthongs, musty ablauts, bilabial fricatives—take shape, I hear her, hear her speaking to me from the background, from the corner of the room she has taken over, from her chair, from the side of the bed where she dips her fingers into a pan of warm water, dips her hands and begins to wash her bruised arms as she sits looking out the window at summer bullying the trees in Washington Square Park; I hear her voice, the monotone, the unvariable persistent elegant phrasing, the complaints and observations probing the air, entering me impersonally, wheedling and begging, commanding, dividing me from myself, whittling new ornaments of feeling we might turn wonderingly in our hands, gauds and trickery, silky shaped phrases for a life, for the day and its merciless divisions, all apparent at once in each word, by now nothing left out between us, nothing without its hidden and its obvious meaning.

And all meanings the same, she might say, lifting her beautiful ruined face to the light, turning toward me, smiling blankly as if I am a picture of myself held up to remind her of what life once was in a place she has forgotten.

2

Washington Square Park. Under the half-red maple, an aging gentleman, just into retirement, sitting rigidly under the constraints of a lifetime's fear of humiliation . . .

. . . I couldn't complain he says, the poet in my book says, I too was spooked by my father's illness. I couldn't stand seeing the cancer eating him up. Disease, failure, great loss, any gross mishap in fact, insane love, even misplaced affection, clumsiness, awkward phrasing, forgetting a date—they could all lead to ostracism. This was the great fear, as always: shunning. Those we loved not speaking to us. It happened all the time. We crossed cadence, fell out of step and the jackals (that is to say our ex-friends and loved ones) devoured us with silence . . .

There's a short line of pear trees between the café and the hospital. They're on the other side of the avenue, across a small park about fifty yards away. The wind in the leaves makes them look as if they are bustling off somewhere. Rae wanted to see the doctor alone. The pain's subsided, and she didn't want me anywhere near while he probed up into her womb.

. . . *after a hot July, August turns cool, fall-like* . . .

"Call me," I say to Benjamin Prang, "and see if you can explain to me what I am doing."

Late August—pools and streaks of sunlight on the uncut grass in the park. Near me a ginkgo, sycamores (plane trees), a disfigured maple, linden, oaks. There's the mossy, mildewy, shitty smell of the dog run beyond the trees. A man in orange jodhpurs walks quickly by. "A grin like a slice from a wheel of sunshine," he says to an invisible companion.

Rae's out.

3

Rae vomits in the bathroom. I sit on the bed sweating. It's heroin she's reacting to, the powder fired and shot into her veins with needles we stole from her father's sickbed on our last trip to Nebraska. She screams for me to come help her, I do, drag her upright, walk her around as we used to walk overdosers around in the sixties, but she can't take it, she's slumping, falling, going limp, vomiting as she walks. I punch the phone, call 911, an ambulance arrives, they strap her in, rush her downstairs (standing her upright in the elevator), roar off to St. Vincent's three blocks away. Medicos pump her stomach, give her a shot, put her to bed and then I get a severe look from the doctor, but he's tired and doesn't have much to say. I sit in the room looking out the window at a brilliant Sunday late-summer day, wind blowing the tops of the pear trees in the little park on Seventh, shaking them like palm fronds. My mind's blank. Either that or it's running so fast I don't know what to think.

4

coxcomb
dahlia
snapdragon
cosmo
zinnia

Park. Late August. Four men playing cards at a picnic table. One of the men, a sallow, worn man with long gray hair slicked in gaps across his freckled skull has a little girl with him. The girl's about eight. She has bushy dark gold hair and watches the game intently. I know this girl: she's deaf and dumb. When her companion grins and makes a gesture of triumph she utters loud bellowing sounds the other men wince and scowl at. The girl doesn't seem to notice.

In my novel, I write about the living dead. My unnamed poet speaks of his life spent among the living dead, but this is only a figure I use, a conceit; there is really no such thing, except in a poetic sense. The rest of us live among the living, no matter how bad they look. Even Rae who is wan and speaks with a twisted mouth, who vomits often and stands at the stove looking into a pot in which milk scum has formed a thick membrane on the surface, who looks without interest or comprehension, even Rae, the woman I love, is alive. She sits on the edge of the bed holding her balled white socks in her hands. "Could you get my works?" she says, "and fix me a picker upper?" I do this. It isn't as hard as I thought it would be, this life. We have money. My books have sold to the movies. Outside a clear autumnal light fills the trees.

. . . Fall begins to ease in, a little early. In the park people still walk slowly; summer amble. "It's so hard for some people to hide their feelings," a woman on the next bench says. "It's almost impossible for me to show my emotions," her companion says.

". . . all the truth you're going to know is in this moment."
"Well, yeah — so what?"

. . . sound of a small plane
— above the West Village

. . . in late afternoon in early fall before the leaves change the tops of trees are golden in the pure full light.

5

I walk up Riverside Drive taking notes for the novel. I'm looking for houses where the poet's family might have lived. He comes from old money. There are many houses, stone usually, slabs of granite showing the comb marks where they were quarried and cut to size. Iron drainpipes, an Osage orange tree, a man in a Hawaiian shirt pissing against a tree. The poet looks through the slim, quavering branches of poplar trees and thinks of how as a child he believed the trees were the remnants of an ancient forest that once stretched unbroken to the North Pole, how he believed for a time when he was six that he could set off into this forest and find his way north into the undiscovered lands where bison and woolly mammoths lived. *As a child*, he thinks, *as a child I imagined . . .*, turning his thoughts away from himself.

Later he runs into a former mistress; there is a surge of electricity between them. They talk, look at each other out of amused eyes—hers amused, his lustful—then they walk together into the park, stop by a tree and kiss. The poet feels the kiss deep in his body. He breaks out in a sweat, gently pushes her away, holds her away to look into her broad suntanned face. She smiles at him. They continue walking.

. . . the living dead: who qualifies?

Jazz festival in the park. Stanley Turrentine plays his saxophone in a group put together for the event. In their first number (another sax, different from Stanley's, piano, drums, bass), each takes a solo turn; the piece is a long series of solos the other members stand back from, courteous, encouraging; the sound drifts like smoke over the treetops, sinks among us on our benches, settles down and stays a while . . .

. . . there's never enough summer.

"There's no other side to grief," Rae says. She stands at the window watching children run past. The children are wearing dark blue military uniforms and they carry yellow paper streamers. There is no way to guess who they are or what they are doing. Rae turns to me; her pale blue eyes are watery with defiance, self-pity and shame, but there is nothing I can do for her. I take the pipe from her fingers, but in a few minutes she will want it back. I've stopped arguing. I go to the other window and we stand there in the tall living room, each at his own window, looking out at the bright remnants of a warm fall day.

"Psychology is for wimps."
— *The New Yorker*

6

Long ago, back when they were hardly more than children, my mother cheated on my father. *Cheated* is not the word (they were not married at the time), but it is a word I have heard used in this context. My mother discovered another side to things. This discovery dazzled and compelled her.

It's later—there's a stillness in the trees before afternoon rain.

I left the park for a few hours, called Rae, told her I was going shopping. "I'm buying a chicken at Jefferson Market," I said. "Do you want anything?" She didn't. She almost never does, except sweets, she gets a craving, buys candy bars by the armload, chocolate in boxes, junk-food items, high-ticket items as well, Jon Vie pastries, crumbly French shells bulging like pumped muscles with cream. She sets these items before her on the table and strips the wrappers off, piles the delectables in a heap before her and selects, takes a bite, puts it down, selects another and bites, works through the heap this way until each bar and pastry has a bite taken out of it. Her fingers are runny and black with chocolate, streaked with cream. "No," she says, "I don't want anything. Unless you could get me some Tabac chocolate."

Around me the drug sellers hawk their wares. *Sess, sess.* (Years ago I thought they were saying *Sex*—and told this to someone at a party, bragging confidentially about my secret knowledge of park lore. He looked at me funny. It was weeks before I discovered my mistake.) Under a thick dust cloud beyond the trees dogs exercise. The drug sellers work very hard. They're out in all weathers. They strut and posture. They argue, shout, tool malicious phrases, brandish bottles occasionally, stamp their feet in anger. They can't afford to go too far, get too upset; it's bad for business. The grim policemen pass on scooters.

My parents didn't break up over Mother's infidelity. My father was crazy about my mother. He stuck with her. My mother honored her word to my father. She left the dazzlement and delight, left the warm afternoons on the sandy banks of the Acton River, left the afternoons in the clearing in the pine woods, the afternoons lying in a deer stand high in a cypress near the old farm road, and returned to my father. She returned and stayed with him for years. My father forgave everything. The first time he did.

7

Capable, energetic, perseverant—yet I stalled out at the deli counter in Jefferson Market, came to a halt among my neighbors, couldn't raise my hand to respond to the deli man's call for number eighty-two, which I clutched in my fingers. The tide of shopping swept past me, tossed up a young man in a burly tweed jacket. I didn't try to call it back.

fatum
refractory
ascesis

My poet rides to Montauk with his nephew, a young man home for the summer from his graduate studies at the Colorado School of Mines.
 . . . but halfway there the nephew changes his mind (about something) and stops at a produce stand on the Amagansett Highway. He says he wants a basket of the early local peaches.
 I waited in the car, but when he didn't come back right away I got out and went looking for him. He was in back, behind the stand, sitting in a wicker armchair drinking a cup of coffee. Beyond him were large flower gardens and beyond the gardens half-plowed fields. There were mallows and zinnias blooming in the gardens, several acres of them. The mallows were red and yellow, some few were white. The zinnias were rainbow colored, slim, stalky, nodding in breeze. Beyond and just as striking were the fields torn to pieces by plows, thick deep green grass turned over exposing the rich red undersoil. Flights of black birds wheeled and dived over the field. We sat in chairs and looked out on this without saying anything. For an hour we stayed there. By the time we roused ourselves we had forgotten what we stopped for. We left without buying anything and without having said a word to one another. Chastened by beauty, pilgrims dumbfounded and released from the mind's intersession.

... waves coming in flat, in a broad sweep that leaves wide stretches of shallow water lacy and white. The ocean beyond has a slightly worked look, but without swells or caps. The early morning sun has coated a wide section from shoreline to horizon glittering white. The sky is pale blue, bleached: a fall sky, with thin streaks and transparent patches of cloud. The sun is warm, but the breeze is cool. Walkers wear sweatshirts over their suits.

Rae sits on the beach with her feet in a hole she's dug. Cold seawater fills the hole. She works her toes into the watery sand, leans forward and spits into the hole, lets the spit drool from her lips. The bright muscled-up wind snatches at her hair, twirls it around her head. Her face is becoming gaunt, her eyes glitter. She is in fact remarkably beautiful; as haggard as she is becoming, even frail, there is no time — I realize this — when she stops being beautiful. It comes to me there will be no time when she becomes repulsive to me. She will be beautiful all the way down. There is nothing in her, nothing about her that repels me.

8

... in the park, lame completely done-in men cough and look wearily around. Like ex-emperors they make signs to trees, to passersby, without speaking. They expect to be understood by the universe. I do, too.

In the novel I quote from my own life, from what I observe. The park is a main stage for the poet's progress. He likes to sit in Washington Square, musing, looking around, taking small notes, transcribing the development and degradation of seasons. I myself come to the park almost every fair afternoon, sit with a few books piled around me, read and take notes, watch the human activity.

I put a letter in the big blue mailbox then stand silently before it, lost in thought until I can't remember whom I have written to, what I am doing standing bareheaded in the sunlight of an October day.

I lock and unlock desk drawers, the poet says, *put nothing in, take nothing out.*

Marigolds, shredded, golden, smelling of medicine, of heroin beginning to cook.

The man at the park urinal, pissing beside me, stares heavily at my cock.

Today, from Pier 41, I watched a man on a houseboat kill, pluck and gut a goose. It was a Canada goose. The man was close enough, I called to him, at first angry at what he was doing, but he said he had raised the goose himself. He was lying, I could tell. He killed the goose as I came up — lifted it by the head and swung it once in the air and slammed it down hard. Instantly as it hit the deck he sliced the head off with a large black knife. Blood spurted and the goose quivered and twitched. The man held it up by the feet, draining blood. He had a large pot boiling on a camp stove and went to this, thrust the goose in and then with a clean rag plucked and wiped the feathers off. Then he gutted the goose with the same knife he used to kill it. He threw the guts over the side.

9

"I dream," Rae says, "that I am a water source. Not a spring in the mountains, but a clear pool in marshy country from which rivers flow."

"Like the Okefenokee," I say, "a bowl of water, from which rivers flow."

"No," she says, "a dream source, small and rounded with indeterminate banks, set in a golden marsh, from which rivers flow endlessly in all directions."

I look out the window at the park. Wind blows harshly through the tree tops. Some of the maples have lost their leaves in the crowns, like old men gone bald.

"I am exhausted, yet inexhaustable," Rae says.

I'm scared to death most of the time, but go on anyway.

10

They filmed in the park today. Children in sportive outfits playing on the swings. The camera, a large beige and black-trimmed apparatus, swung in close to the faces of four year olds riding a slide-bar swing. Just offstage parents stroked their lounging, restless off-duty child actors like cats. A child in a blue blazer and untied tennis shoes threw rocks at pigeons. The parents have expectant looks on their faces, like hungry people about to be fed.

As I was sitting on my bench watching this a small white pigeon landed on the armrest next to me. An old man in a shabby leather overcoat sitting on the other side of me leaned over and indicating the pigeon said, "White death." I nodded and grinned. I had the feeling we were both auditioning.

11

. . . in the sculpture garden, by the café bar on the roof of the Metropolitan Museum, a gleaming gold pest strip clotted with dead and dying honey bees.

As he looks intently at Monet's water lilies a small boy pisses down his bare leg.

Rae sometimes speaks in tongues. My mother, in her middle age, would gibber; driven into her madness, stalled there like a convoy in the jungle, she ran her engines wildly all night. Rae speaks out of her nod, shouts, cries out, offers soliloquies in the dark.

. . . sound of distant thunder. I'm not always sure, in the city, whether the rumbling sound I hear is really thunder.

Every afternoon an older woman brings her aged parents to the park. The three of them sit on a bench together and the oldsters feed seed to the pigeons. The birds gather thickly on the ground before them. They perch on their knees, in their laps, on their arms. The old man, a wizened killer in a plaid cap, is very serious, but the old woman, another killer, grins like a happy child. The daughter gets into it too, but not as deeply. She tears bits of a roll, tosses them well out in front of her.

. . . famous in the *villas miserias*
(vizas m . . .)
(shanty towns) of Buenos Aires

Oct. 10 — at dusk, crickets in St. Luke's garden . . .

12

Outside our house this morning (when I came out and stalled—no, not stalled—drifted out, to loiter among the sounds, to watch the water truck pass . . .) outside our house this morning I discover Spaniards and aged Chinese gentlemen. The Spaniards argue a point of metaphysics, while the Chinese gents shake out sheets of newspaper to free them of dust and crumbs, spread them on the stoop and sit down. The sun, as they speak and work, turns the rims and cornices, the tilted balconies of the apartment building across the street gold.

"Mine has always been a story of redemption, of the necessary comeback."
When I turn to see who's spoken, there's a well-dressed man standing with a beautiful red-headed woman. They look like models posing for each other, and themselves, look like areas of perfection, a roped-off section of humanity, a display of potential realized, not sufferers.
"If you looked at me from a distance," the man says, "you might say my life was caught in an updraft, climbing always, a rising progress, but my story, to me, has been a story of failure, of loss . . . redeemed. Over and over I get saved, lifted up. My fate as I saw it was in the necessary comeback, a return from a psychic deadzone that I inadvertently fell into. In great and small ways this was so. Whether it was a waiter's rudeness that sparked a retaliation I later had to atone for, or my own child's death, I was scrambling for a hold in my life, a way to live with a little grace. Of course those who know my work know this already—or already know that the tension between appearance and fact is my subject. I have pursued this without irony. I was successful from the beginning."
Just now, as I write this, a man beneath the café window steps through a bank of blossoming begonias and shakes his fist at a woman walking by. The woman sneers at him. "Nantucket!" the man screams at her, and again, "Nantucket!"

The Spanish and Chinese gentlemen have been replaced by Eastern Europeans, by Poles and Czechs, by repressed Moldavian intellectuals who shake their heads viciously in disagreement with everything that's said. Artists' wives, baggage handlers, interrupted former child actors drift by. Detached black men, their mothers' favorites, sway like irises under the heavy sunlight. A pale woman with mad black hair, a gypsy queen, down at the end of the street, shrieks wildly at nothing anyone can see.

The problem with believing in the power of irony is the faith it forces us to put into the notion of cause and effect. The tremendous investment we must then make in the *purely rational*.

mantic
lucent
abulia

When I meet someone, I wait — it takes a while — I let them become friends first — sometimes this takes months (occasionally years) — I never stop thinking about it, but don't mention, in the early days, or even after we begin to share certain obvious confidences such as why we have no children, how much money we made last year, the scar where a lover bit the ball of a thumb to the bone, I don't speak up about my parents, don't say that after years of acquiescence, after years of a moldering, desperate vitality and curtailment, of service, of works collected, of what my sister and I took as love, my father, on a sunny afternoon in early spring, murdered my mother and then killed himself.

Two Poems by William Logan

The Quicksand Builders

The quicksand builders built
against the Folly of All.
They built from ancient custom.
They built for the good of the Wall.

As fast as they built, it sank,
and as fast as it sank, they built.
They felt no loss or sorrow
or residue of guilt.

As long as they stayed on the job
there was hope that the job would go.
The common people knelt
and prayed to the gods below.

The builders knew no gods
could save like a hard bed of silt,
and as fast as they built, it sank,
and as fast as it sank, they built.

Eden in the Dustbowl

She was her own celestial city now.
The ravens and the crows in residence
were fallen angels of the picket fence.
Behind it stood the Devil's Jersey cow.
Each dawn a cold, forbidding sun still rose.
The dishes were still there to put away,

but something different—well, she couldn't say.
Perhaps it was the closet full of clothes.
How could she know what true confession was?
Two squalling kids, a husband on the make,
and that June evening with the coral snake—
a devil is not paid for what he does.
There, there in the clearing was the golden bough.
She stood amid the garbage with her sow.

Two Poems by Sarah Lindsay

Lungfish Conquers Depression

Where the bladderwort and water lily
give way to bulrushes and pickerelweed
and cattail heads nod hugely high,
every day for a thousand thousand
she keeps her eyes in the pond,
under the wind. Everything here
is as cool as everything else.
In the filtered visibility
she can set her chin in the muck
and submit her gills to the endless wet feed,
her skin to the close, slack hold all over.
No questions. Everything here is here.
Now and now and now.

She doesn't know
why this time she pushes past the surface tension
and wimples up the minute incline
on jellied stumps. She doesn't know
how far to the loblolly pines or what they are.
How heavy her body, wobbling on the peat
without support, in a shower of dry infrared.
So many edges. She feels a pocket
flex inside her neck, she gapes
at the scoured entry of demanding air.

Neanderthal

Walking home from my powerless car
I pass through a dozen supper smells, each
more promising than anything I've ever cooked.
But then my neighbors long since left me behind.
They know just how to use sage and cumin.
They change their own spark plugs, prune shrubs and feed
  roses.
In that garage a woman is caning a chair,
tight straw stars. My chin recedes,
my knuckles scrape the street I'm crossing.

My skills come from the wrong past.
I know how, in a team of two,
to bring down a marriage heavy with years,
cut out its tongue and liver, flay the skin,
break its mastodon limbs across
and suck the bitter marrow;
you can last a while like that.
I know how to forage.
I know how to sleep in the cold.

Three Poems by Andrew Hudgins

Heaven

Between my back fence and the drainage ditch,
the county's
            no-man's land, I'd
been chopping brush and forking out
thick roots,
            expanding my garden, a little
                                    extra space
for bush beans and
            some okra. Had been.
But now I've stopped.
                  A copperhead
is striking at
            my boots, a light
                              tap, tap
tap, tap
      that I can barely feel.
I don't move. Watch.
                  I watch.
                        I've armored myself
in long pants, work
                  gloves, heavy boots
against
      this weaponed patch of wilderness:
thorns, yellow jackets, nettles, poison oak,
and wild
      blackberry canes — the
                        serpent's Eden,
the copperhead's paradise,
                  which he defends
poetically
      as his harsh heaven is

stripped, tilled, raked level, hoed into furrows,
                                                    planted.
The brown head
                  strikes and strikes my boot,
till,
      with the hoe, I hook
                              the angry snake
and flick it,
              writhing, across the ditch
into my neighbor's untouched bramble
where all
          the squirrels, rabbits, mice
                                        have fled
from my
        blade, my advancing paradise.

Jacob

In the rose and pale gold of
                              declining light
I brace my stiff feet on dry leaves, and grasp
the trunk
          of a green oak. Embracing it,
I sway, yield to its
                    tough-limber stem.
                                        Then, looser,
I push,
       pump, pull,
                   wrestling with a rough, sprightly
young oak, thick as my wrist and twelve feet high.
It pushes back.
                It loves a tussle! Clear sap
wells from the river back, taproot, and trunk,
and tingles through
                    my body, toe
                                 to crown,

and soon
        I launch out, swing,
                sway, bending
the young tree, dipping it
in grace-
      less dancing till it springs back, dips me
and flips me on the ground.
                I rise, take hold
once more
        and wrestle till it blesses me,
and the virtue thereof
            passes from the oak
to me. Or
        maybe we exchange. Maybe
the oak absorbs my aches, un-
              gracious glooms,
leakages, and lethargy.
              I shout and sing.
I lash my gray skin scarlet with a branch,
put on my black suit and my broad-brimmed hat,
and limp home in the freshly fallen dark.

Goat

Though reverence may not save us
we must carry ourselves
with reverence.
           A song
at pale twilight of love
and mourning fills our eyes
with easy, pleasing tears
and suspect judgment, until
malicious laughter erupts
inside the song.
           At noon

a piping from deep shadow—
even in the city
a piping from green tangles
of boxwood and honeysuckle,
a haunted piping: the mind
drifts and we dreamily
search upward for the moon,
then quickly walk away,
head down and face averted,
followed by judgmental
laughter, malign delight.
You may shake your head
and say *no*,
                but the goat god's quick
to fix his gaze and quick
to follow it. A flurry
of hoofbeats along
the edge of shadow. A glimpse
in tittering oak leaves
of the monster's dreamy smile,
the god's angelic
dissipated face,
and we desert the road,
forsake the fresh-turned furrow
and enter, mesmerized,
his green circle, the green
enveloping dream he dreams
for us.
        Does reverence
guard us from the god's
quick eye, or draw it? He throws
himself on sheep and shepherd,
goat and goatherd, you,
me, him, and her,
and we, against our choosing,
receive his august gifts.
Strange babies, hairy and sly,
are dropping from our wives

and daughters. Strange lambs, their eyes
alight with god-fire, unfold
from our indifferent sheep.
In pastures, near the barn,
by the wedding bed, above
the moist gray deathbed, we hear
from greenery the goat
god laughing — laughing because we laugh,
laughing because we have
stopped laughing, laughing and laughing
because we cannot laugh.

Brian Culhane

Knowing Greek
for Hazard Adams

Once it seemed possible, those boys
Peeking out of gun slits at the German line
Or on graves detail, wet, miserable,
Oblivious to the dawn's miserable joys.
I hardly know what to say to their faces
Locked away in the secret history of the war,
The Great one, which everyone knows was lost,
Really lost, at Versailles. Sure, I could go
To pastured no-man's-land, yet another
In a shambling line of the misinformed,
Staring, too ready to honor landscape.
What have we learned? A teacher's question.
Russell's *Principia Mathematica* proved false,
No doubt, and the decades have never ceased
From accelerating to where I now sit
In the Elgin Room ("De Greeks were Godes!"
Shouted Fuseli at first seeing the marbles),
Contemplating the beauty that brought Byron
To fight for liberty against the Turks
—Broken by marsh fever at Missolonghi,
His valet Fletcher still with him. Shelley,
Legend has it, drowned with a Greek play
Stuck in a pocket. "We are all Greeks," he said.
In Rome, you can see the piazza where
His friend's sheets burned. Keats had no Greek.
He wrote his sonnet to Chapman's Homer
Out of ardor for an epic Englished.
For him, too, breathing and Greek came together,
If only as absence, some swift final pain.

"Yes, on to Pi, / When the end loomed nigh"
— So Hardy's newly dead Liddell to long dead Scott
On their alphabetical quest, and I
Look again at the forms the good Lord saved
To steal and bury in this London sanctuary.
Athanatos, deathless; *psuche*, soul: engraved
On my mind since ephebe days at City College
Where I copied out my own slim lexicon.
Marathon may be more important than Hastings
"Even as an event in English history" (Mill),
But noting the shortness of their upper lips,
Carlyle vexed the painter Watts by claiming
Pheidias's sculpted men lacked "cleverness."

Yes. Once it seemed possible, those boys
With their classical educations bursting
Like gods from mud, kissing reddening stones
Still redder under a pockmarked plain.
All those undying souls writing home
As the first mechanized war stole their words,
As *lads* became *men*, and *honour* came to what?
You're never so right as when you're dead,
The marbles seem to say; or with Peleus to his son,
Always be the champion; or, with Weil,
Force is any X that makes a thing out of a mortal
— A sudden frieze of centuries gone wrong.
In marmoreal light I raise a chastened hand:
Beauty is truth, a sick youth's equation.
Trenches lie on the surface of my palm.

whispered wetly in his ear. "Dolce Vita for the big race on Sunday, hear me? Raffi Sabbato bought the jockeys. All of them, hear me? Don't tell anyone."

"Mickie, I hear you loud and clear, and Raffi was in my shop this morning but you weren't, which was a pity because there's a nice dinner jacket there waiting for you to try it on. Now sit down, please, like a good friend."

Out of the corner of his eye, Pendel saw two large men in chauffeurs suits advancing along the edge of the room. Pendel reached a protective arm halfway across Mickie's mountainous shoulders.

"Mickie, if you make any more trouble I'll never cut another suit for you," he said in English. And in Spanish to the two men: "We're all fine, thank you, gentlemen. Mr Abraxas will be leaving of his own accord, thank you."

Mickie Abraxas, Pendel explained, without Osnard asking. Father a Greek shipowner and chum of General Omar Torrijos. Torrijos had him reorganise Panama's drug trade for the Americans, turn it into something everyone could be proud of in the war against Communism.

A manuscript page from The Tailor of Panama.

John le Carré

The Art of Fiction CXLIX

John le Carré was born in Poole, England, on October 19, 1931. He had a gloomy childhood, thanks to the disruptive motions of his father, an erratic businessman who kept the family moving from place to place. After attending a series of private English schools, le Carré was called upon for national service and spent several years in Vienna with the Army Intelligence Corps. When the term expired, he returned to England and enrolled at Lincoln College, Oxford. Graduation was followed by a procession of odd jobs, including one year in which he taught at Eton.

In 1960, le Carré, whose real name is David John Moore Cornwell, resumed his intelligence career with the Foreign Service. During this time he began writing novels, the first entitled Call for the Dead. *His second book,* A Murder of Quality, *appeared in 1962 while le Carré was stationed at the British Embassy in Bonn. Two years later he resigned from the Foreign Service to devote himself entirely to writing. He achieved international fame as the author of* The Spy Who Came in from the Cold. *His later books include* A Small Town in Germany; Tinker, Tailor, Soldier, Spy; Smiley's People; The Little Drummer Girl; A Perfect Spy; The Russia House *and* Our Game, *almost all of which have been adapted for movies and television.*

The interview took place in the auditorium of New York's YMHA on a late autumn day in 1996. Le Carré had arrived from London earlier that day to promote the publication of his sixteenth novel, The Tailor of Panama. *The auditorium was packed. After the interview he cheerfully submitted to questioning by the crowd, then moved to an adjoining space where autograph-seekers, some carrying more than a dozen books, had formed a long queue that curled around the room. Le Carré, who likes to turn in early, looked fatigued. He stayed on until almost midnight, ministering to each request in a broad, legible hand.*

INTERVIEWER

Can you say something about your early reading?

JOHN LE CARRÉ

I grew up in a completely bookless household. It was my father's boast that he had never read a book from end to end.

I don't remember any of his ladies being bookish. So I was entirely dependent on my schoolteachers for my early reading with the exception of *The Wind in the Willows*, which a stepmother read to me when I was in hospital. My earliest reading included Maugham, the heroic English storytellers, Henty, Sapper, Peter Cheyney and, thank heaven, the great and wonderful Conan Doyle. I graduated joyously to Dickens and erratically to Bernard Shaw and Galsworthy. And cautiously to the heavy contemporaries, Koestler, Gide and Camus. But the big explosion in my reading occurred in my late teens when I was seduced by the German muse. I devoured the whole of German literature alive, as it seems to me now. I have probably read more German literature than I have English. Today my pleasure is with nineteenth-century storytellers: Balzac, Dickens and the rest.

INTERVIEWER

And among contemporary writers?

LE CARRÉ

Everything by Marquez, and sudden batches of new writers. Most recently, practically everything by Beryl Bainbridge, just for the pleasure of her ear. I read most between books, and very little fiction while I am writing.

INTERVIEWER

You taught at Eton for a while. What did you teach, and was your stay there of any value to your writing?

LE CARRÉ

I taught principally German language and literature at Eton. But any master with private pupils must be prepared to teach anything they ask for. That can be as diverse as the early paintings of Salvador Dalí or how bumblebees manage to fly. Eton is a place of extremes, and these were good for me as a writer. The English upper classes can be seen at their best and worst. The good pupils are often brilliant, and they keep you on your toes and take you to the limits of your knowledge. The worst pupils provide a unique insight into the criminal mind. On all these counts my time at Eton provided me with riches. I even set one early novel in a school that was quite like Eton: *A Murder of Quality*.

INTERVIEWER

Why did you change your name?

LE CARRÉ

When I began writing, I was what was politely called "a foreign servant." I went to my employers and said that I'd written my first novel. They read it and said they had no objections, but even if it were about butterflies, they said, I would have to choose a pseudonym. So then I went to my publisher, Victor Gollancz, who was Polish by origin, and he said, "My advice to you, old fellow, is choose a good Anglo-Saxon couple of syllables. Monosyllables." He suggested something like Chunk-Smith. So as is my courteous way, I promised to be Chunk-Smith. After that, memory eludes me and the lie takes over. I was asked so many times why I chose this ridiculous name; then the writer's imagination came to my help. I saw myself riding over Battersea Bridge, on top of a bus, looking down at a tailor's shop. Funnily enough, it *was* a tailor's shop, because I had a terrible obsession about buying clothes in order to become a diplomat in Bonn. And it *was* called something of this sort—*le Carré*. That satisfied everybody for years. But lies don't last with age. I find a frightful compulsion towards truth these days. And the truth is, I don't know.

INTERVIEWER

Which intelligence service were you in?

LE CARRÉ

Even now, some residual sense of loyalty prevents me from talking much about it. I entered the secret world when I was young. I kind of lurched into it. There never seemed an alternative. I was first picked up when I was a young student in Bern, having run away from my first school. I retained what is politely called "a reporting responsibility." Then, for my military service, I went to Austria. That was a very formative time, because one of my jobs was trolling through the displaced-persons camps, looking for people who were fake refugees, or for people whose circumstances were so attractive to us from an intelligence point of view that we might consider returning them, with their consent, to the countries they came from. For a person of, as I was then, barely twenty-one, it was an immense responsibility at an extraordinary moment in history, which, horrible as it was, I was very pleased to have shared. Afterwards, after teaching at Eton, I went into the cold-war setup properly. In all I don't suppose that I spooked around for more than seven or eight years, and that's forty years ago, but that was my little university for the purposes that I needed later to write. I think that if I'd gone to sea at that time I would have written about the sea. If I'd gone into advertising or stockbroking, that would have been my stuff. It was from there that I began abstracting and peopling my other world, my alternative, private world, which became my patch, and it became a Tolkien-like operation, except that none of my characters have hair between their toes.

INTERVIEWER

Was there a moment during all of this when you really felt that you were going to write about it?

LE CARRÉ

There was. I had the curious and very rewarding example when I was in the first of the two services that I joined of working with a man called John Bingham, whose real name was Lord Clanmorris. He was a thriller writer, and also an extremely good intelligence officer, a moleish, tubby fellow. He gave me not only the urge to write, but also a kind of outline of George Smiley, which I later filled in from other sources, notably my own. He and a don at Oxford who I knew very well became parts of this composite character called Smiley.

INTERVIEWER

Did you find it easy? Did you have great confidence in yourself as a writer?

LE CARRÉ

I have a great debt of gratitude to the press for this. In those days English newspapers were much too big to read on the train, so instead of fighting with my colleagues for the *Times*, I would write in little notebooks. I lived a long way out of London. The line has since been electrified, which is a great loss to literature. In those days it was an hour and a half each way. To give the best of the day to your work is most important. So if I could write for an hour and a half on the train, I was already completely jaded by the time I got to the office to start work. And then there was a resurgence of talent during the lunch hour. In the evening something again came back to me. I was always very careful to give my country second-best.

INTERVIEWER

What sorts of things were you writing in these little notebooks?

LE CARRÉ

I was writing the very first book, without any kind of skeleton, without any conscious model, but with this odd character, George Smiley, to go along with me. I've never been able to write a book without one very strong character in my rucksack. The moment I had Smiley as a figure, with that past, that memory, that uncomfortable private life and that excellence in his profession, I knew I had something I could live with and work with.

INTERVIEWER

Do you always start with this image of character, rather than, say, plot?

LE CARRÉ

Yes, usually somebody. In fact, I can't remember setting off on my travels without some picture of a character to take with me. It really is a companion. I was traveling once in northeast Laos to write a book called *The Honourable Schoolboy*, and I got stuck up with the journalist David Greenway. We had to make a frightful journey to somewhere, and he turned to me and said, "Which class would Smiley travel?" So I said he would definitely be in that one with the wonderful washing urns and all of that—he'd mix with the natives. Greenway said, "I'll tell you what we'll do: we'll put Smiley in there and we'll travel first-class."

INTERVIEWER

You have a wonderful story about the germination of *The Spy Who Came in from the Cold*.

LE CARRÉ

That's right. At that time I was very caught up in the cold war in Germany. I was stationed in Bonn, going to Berlin a lot, and that was the crucible of all that spy commerce in those days. One of my jobs at the embassy, one of my day jobs, you might say, was bringing over German dignitaries, introducing them to British politicians, and functioning as interpreter. I was sitting alone in London Airport, minding my own business, when a very rough-edged, kind of Trevor Howard figure, walked in and sat himself at the bar beside me. He fished in his pocket, put down a great handful of change in heaven-knows-which currencies and denominations, and then said, "A large scotch." Between him and the barman, they just sorted out the money. He drank the scotch and left. I thought I picked up a very slight Irish accent. And that was really all, but there was a deadness in the face, and he looked, as we would have said in the spy world in those days, as if he'd had the hell posted out of him. It was the embodiment, suddenly, of somebody that I'd been looking for. It was he, and I never spoke to him, but he was my guy, Alec Leamas, and I knew he was going to die at the Berlin Wall.

INTERVIEWER

What happens then? You have your character; what process follows?

LE CARRÉ

The process is empathy, fear and dramatization. I have to put him into conflict with something, and that conflict usually comes from within. They're usually people who are torn in some way between personal and institutional loyalty. Then there's external conflict. "The cat sat on the mat" is not the beginning of a story, but "The cat sat on the dog's mat" *is*. I take him with me, and I know his habits and manners. I take my tailor to Panama, not knowing anything about the place, and immediately plunge myself into the rag trade, the clothing business. Speaking for my man, Harry Pendel, I inquire all over the place. What would be the chances of setting up a bespoke tailoring business to make really smart suits? I went so far as to visit estate agents and look at potential shops. I talked to the big wholesalers, who said, "Yes, possibly, for bespoke tailoring, if you could invent the taste in Panama, and you could really win people away from buying Armani suits, then it would work. If it became the fashion, if it became the rage, if suddenly in the Union Club in Panama it was impossible to be seen without a Pendel & Braithwaite suit, it would work." So without actually buying the place and buying the stock, I get as realistic an appraisal of the possibilities of his life as I can. I go and find a house for him. I decided to marry him to a Zonian, who's a kind of hybrid of American and Panamanian, a woman who'd been brought up in the Canal Zone, but who was American by sentiment and culture and birth. I took the trouble to mix with people with that kind of background. But I was very much doing Harry's job for him, and I don't think that writers have much center, really. I feel much more like an actor looking for a part. I put on Pendel's clothes in my own mind. Similarly, if I'm some other character, if I'm in the previous book, which was also partly set in Panama, if I'm an old Brit spy waiting for his joe, his agent, to turn up at the Continental Hotel in Panama, then I'll spend a few hours doing his job, watching the people go by, trying internally to evoke the tension of that moment. "Is it he, is it he? Who is it? Can't see . . ." and so on.

INTERVIEWER

Does your wife worry about these communion-like experiences?

LE CARRÉ

She's pretty used to it. It's better than being married to one person.

INTERVIEWER

Does anybody help you with the research? Do you have an assistant?

LE CARRÉ

I try, as in the spy trade, to find a really good local contact. Sometimes it's a journalist; in this case, it was an American novelist of distinction called Richard Koster, who lives in Panama. Dick and I became buddies. He marked my card a good deal, said, "These are the people to talk to." And then after that you start leapfrogging. I meet *you* through Dick, and you say, "Well, the chap you should really talk to is so-and-so." Six people down the line you find yourself sitting with an arms dealer in a nightclub, and somebody's really talking about himself. The thing is, if you are a good listener and not adversarial, people love to talk about themselves.

INTERVIEWER

Do you make tape recordings?

LE CARRÉ

No, I have a notebook, but all the notes I take are subjective, so that even the notes will be about the characters. Good lines will be given to the characters; they don't just exist as plain lines. So there's some kind of constant interaction between the fantasy that I brought with me to the location—the place as character—and what happens to me after that, the way the fantasy takes on some semblance of truth. What we want is not authenticity; it is credibility. In order to be credible, you have to dress the thing in clothes of authenticity.

INTERVIEWER

How much control do you have over the characters? Does the book ever take completely unexpected turns?

LE CARRÉ

All the turns are unexpected because I never impose much on the plot. Once I had Pendel and his Zonian wife and the baddie coming into the shop, I was as nervous and excited about what would happen as I hope the reader is. I don't have charts and so forth. Like a moviemaker, I have a vision of what the audience will see as they leave the theater, what will be the last image in their heads. In this case, it's the conflagration of Panama. I knew when I started playing with the satire of Panama and that wayward, extraordinary war that the United States fought there—ultimately for good reasons, but initially for very bad ones—that I wanted that to be repeated. I wanted a cycle of history to occur. When you're my age, you have the feeling sometimes that you're seeing the show come round again. For all the flailing and huffing and puffing, there is a kind of fatality about the process of warmaking and the excuses we find for it, the consolation of belligerence in politics.

INTERVIEWER

There's a very different tone in *The Tailor of Panama*, isn't there.

LE CARRÉ
It's much bouncier. I've got more than one string to my bow, and I thought I'd give this one a twang. If you see the world as gloomily as I see it, the only thing to do is laugh or shoot yourself. My guy does both.

INTERVIEWER
It has been said the book mirrors what you feel about England at the moment.

LE CARRÉ
While abroad, I don't want to talk gloomily about my country. I've become interested recently not in the macro-interpretation of my country, but the micro-interpretation. I live in a tiny, desolate part of England, where the real effects of what I see as terrible misgovernment — central misgovernment — can be felt in detail upon agriculture, fishing, communication and transport, all of those things. My definition of a decent society is one that first of all takes care of its losers, and protects its weak. What I see in my country, progressively over these years, is that the rich have got richer, the poor have got poorer. The rich have become indifferent through a philosophy of greed, and the poorer have become hopeless because they're not properly cared for. That's actually something that is happening in many western societies. Your own, I am told, is not free from it. It's certainly something one could see in process in the microcosm of Panama. There are vastly rich people there. Insiders will tell you that the country is still run by about thirty people, people who generate huge wealth and carve the thing up between themselves. Yet it's a brand-new country from lunchtime on the thirty-first of December, 1999. It will have total independence, having been a colony under the Colombians, the French and the Americans. The canal will revert to their own possession. And we have the fascinating sight of a small country identifying itself, finding out who it will be. All sorts of people are waiting for a slice of the cake. Despite appalling unemployment and an appalling poverty

record, they have it within their grasp to even out their society. But by what method is anyone's guess. I tried to play one perception of the country against my own domestic concerns.

INTERVIEWER

Did you have this attitude before you began your research in Panama?

LE CARRÉ

It was something that dawned on me years earlier, actually. I went to Panama seven or eight years ago just to write one passage for *The Night Manager*. There was a drug dealer in that book who was buying arms, and there was a British arms dealer who was selling him the arms. When I was in Miami I asked the drug-enforcement people and the arms-control people where one would go to negotiate these transactions, and they said with one voice, "Panama. Go to the Free Zone of Colon. You can buy and sell anything you want." I said, "What about a firepower demonstration?" and they said, "That's fine, just go up to the Costa Rican border. Everybody does it there."

INTERVIEWER

What does that mean—tanks and F-16s?

LE CARRÉ

Whatever you wanted. You can buy a little quiet, everyone will be cleared out of the area, and then you can do what you want. After meeting a number of arms dealers and people like that, I had a sense of the very venal nature of Panama. I think they're trying to work on it, to get their act together for independence. What I saw was a Casablanca without heroes, and I thought I had to come back. But then I experienced the delight of recognizing that it—the country, I mean—was writing its own ticket for the year 2000. And the whole farce of the last American colony being handed over—we colonial Brits know what that means. The comedy built into that is irresistible.

INTERVIEWER

So you did not have trouble finding adversarial situations for your heroes after the cold war.

LE CARRÉ

No, I really loved it. I'm not saying that I made the transition easily. I think I stumbled a couple of times. All sorts of things that I'd got too used to were taken away. But I never wanted to write about Smiley again. I felt it was done, and I don't like writing through an old man's eyes. You know, the older you get, the younger you want to be. Also, I didn't want to go back to that morbid face-off — I mean my stories were getting frozen into the ice. All of a sudden everything was up for grabs. It was extremely comic that the uninformed were saying that spying is over, hence le Carré is over. The one thing you can bet is that spying is never over. Spying is like the wiring in this building: it's just a question of who takes it over and switches on the lights. It will go on and on and on.

INTERVIEWER

But is espionage not different since the end of the cold war? Do you still keep in touch with spies?

LE CARRÉ

I have a few people, Americans mainly, some Israelis. The Brits don't talk to me. It's necessary to understand what real intelligence work is. It will never cease. It's absolutely essential that we have it. At its best, it is simply the left arm of healthy governmental curiosity. It brings to a strong government what it needs to know. It's the collection of information, a journalistic job, if you will, but done in secret. All the rest of it — intervention, destabilization, assassination, all that junk — is in my view not only anticonstitutional but unproductive and silly. You can never foresee the consequences. But it's a good job as long as intelligence services collect sensible information and report it to their governments, and as long as that intelligence is properly used, thought about and evaluated. Then you come to the question of targets of intelligence: what are the proper targets of the CIA? That's a policy problem. For me, they are much more widespread than you would suppose. I think they should be extended to the ecology, to the pollution of rivers and those things. There is, for example, one plant in northern Russia that disseminates more pollution than the whole of Scandinavia. One plant alone. I think things of that sort are so life-threatening that they should be included in the CIA's brief. And counterterrorism: you cannot make a case for not spying on terrorist organizations. You've got to spy the hell out of them. But countersubversion—that's a really murky target. That is when a government defines what political thoughts are poisonous to the nation, and I find that a terribly dangerous area. And then of course the maverick weapons—they've been left all over the place, partly by us. I mean, where are the Stingers we gave to the Afghans? Also, if you meddle in people's affairs, you then have to live with the consequences. Look at Afghanistan. We recruited the Muslim extremist movement to assist us in the fight against Russia, and we let loose a demon. Intervention is a very dangerous game, and it always has consequences, and they are almost always embarrassing.

INTERVIEWER

Which is the best of the secret services?

LE CARRÉ

You know, it's a bit like schoolmastering: you can never quite tell how good the next chap is. You never see your colleagues at work. If you get one good source—while the CIA and the British had Penkovsky, for example, they had acres of absolutely wonderful material, and they were putting it out under different source-names, for reasons of security—then you look absolutely great to your paymasters. But when Penkovsky ended, suddenly they were all dressed up and had nowhere to go. They looked awful. I am sure that the best intelligence services must still be Israel's. They've made awful

"The Paris Review remains the single most important little magazine this country has produced."

—T. Coraghessan Boyle

THE PARIS REVIEW

Enclosed is my check for:

☐ $34 for 1 year (4 issues)

(All payment must be in U.S. funds. Postal surcharge of $10 per 4 issues outside USA)

☐ Send me information on becoming a *Paris Review* Associate.

Bill this to my Visa/MasterCard:
Sender's full name and address needed for processing credit cards.

_____
Card number   Exp. date

☐ New subscription   ☐ Renewal subscription
☐ New address

Name _____
Address _____
City _____ State _____ Zip code _____

Please send gift subscription to:
Name _____
Address _____
City _____ State _____ Zip code _____
Gift announcement signature _____
call (718)539-7085

Please send me the following:

☐ The Paris Review T-Shirt ($15.00)
  Color _____ Size _____ Quantity _____
☐ The following back issues: Nos. _____
  See listing at back of book for availability.

Name _____
Address _____
City _____ State _____ Zip code _____

☐ Enclosed is my check for $ _____
☐ Bill this to my Visa/MasterCard:

_____
Card number   Exp. date

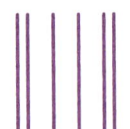

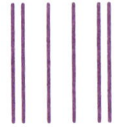

No postage
stamp necessary
if mailed in the
United States

BUSINESS REPLY MAIL
FIRST CLASS   PERMIT NO. 3119   FLUSHING, N.Y.

POSTAGE WILL BE PAID BY ADDRESSEE

THE PARIS REVIEW
45-39 171 Place
FLUSHING NY   11358-9892

No postage
stamp necessary
if mailed in the
United States

BUSINESS REPLY MAIL
FIRST CLASS   PERMIT NO. 3119   FLUSHING, N.Y.

POSTAGE WILL BE PAID BY ADDRESSEE

THE PARIS REVIEW
45-39 171 Place
FLUSHING NY   11358-9892

mistakes, as intelligence services will, but that's because Mossad and Shin Bet are splendidly motivated. If Israel loses a battle, it loses the war; if it loses the war, it loses its country. Everybody in Israel knows what security means, and everybody pulls together. There is no political division between the parties on the subject of security, not until you get to the anguished problems of settlements and so forth. So they are not only the best, and have a very long tradition of being so, but they're the best-motivated. It's much harder now to evaluate the Brits or the Americans or anyone else. As I say, I know next to nothing about the Brits, but what I do hear is that they're far better than they used to be.

INTERVIEWER

Did you know Philby?

LE CARRÉ

No, I didn't. Philby was my secret sharer who I never met. By the time I went into the secret world, as I now know, Philby had passed my name to his Russian controllers. It's a very curious feeling to know that every halfway-perilous thing one did was already known to the Russians miles ahead. I mean I know that good men are scarce. I did not do anything very dangerous or brave. The older you get, the braver you get. I wasn't very brave. And no, I didn't know Philby. When I went to Moscow for the first time, in 1987, I met a man called Gendrik Borovik who said, "There's a very good friend of mine, excellent patriot from your country who would like to meet with you. His name is Kim Philby." I said, "Gendrik, you can't possibly do that to me. I'm going to the ambassador's for dinner tomorrow night. I can't be the guest of the queen's ambassador one night, and the queen's biggest traitor the next. It won't do."

INTERVIEWER

I'm surprised you could resist it.

LE CARRÉ

I know, it was tough to resist, but I did. The invitation was renewed and I still wouldn't go. Then a British journalist, Phil Knightly, went and saw Philby right at the end of his life. Philby knew he was dying. Knightly said, "What do you think of le Carré?" Philby replied, "I don't know. I quite like the books, but the fellow doesn't care for me. He must know something about me." So I puzzled about that. And I think in fact I did know something about him. Kim Philby had a monstrous father, St. John Philby, who ended up selling Rolls-Royces to King Fahd in Saudi Arabia and acting as his advisor. He became a Muslim convert and had a couple of wives—two or three. In fact, I think Fahd gave him a wife. He became a very powerful, unpleasant and anti-British figure in our peculiar empire. Kim grew up under this tyrannous old monster, and when Kim was twelve or thirteen, his father gave him to the Bedouin to be turned into a man. Kim went off into the desert. This was a boy who then went to English public school. I think that the cumulative effect of having such a ferocious father, and a mother he barely knew, produced in him some kind of natural dissenting nature. Indeed he became a subvert. I think he really carried, metaphorically, a pistol in his pocket for the whole of society. If anything embraced him, he wanted to kill it.

I went through a comparable, though perhaps less vicious version of that with my own peculiar papa, who was in and out of prison. He was tremendously dominating. I too had no mother through those years. I felt, thinking about Philby and his father, and myself and my father, that there could have been a time when I, if properly spoken to by the right wise man or woman, could have been seduced into some kind of underground act of revenge against society.

INTERVIEWER

Now that you no longer write on the train to London, what is your working day like?

LE CARRÉ

Well, I still don't type. I write by hand, and my wife types everything up, endlessly, repeatedly. I correct by hand too. I am an absolute monk about my work. It's like being an athlete: you have to find out which are the best hours of the day. I'm a morning person. I like to drink in the evening, go to sleep on a good idea and wake up with the idea solved or advanced. I believe in sleep. And I go straight to work, often very early. If a book's getting to the end of its run, I'll start at four-thirty or five o'clock in the morning and go through to lunchtime. In the afternoon I'll take a walk, and then, over a scotch, take a look at what Jane's typed out, and fiddle with it a bit more. But I always try to go to sleep before I finish working, just a little bit before. Then I know where I'll go the next morning, but I won't quite know what I am going to do when I go. And then in the morning it seems to deliver the answer.

For the last few years I have lived only in the deep country. I've always kept away from writers and the literary set. I'd much rather talk to the woodcutter than a fellow writer. I like the primary material. I don't like exchanging ideas much. I don't like talking about my work, believe it or not. I'm a total bore, actually.

INTERVIEWER

With this monkish routine, how many words do you produce each day?

LE CARRÉ

I don't know. When it's going well it goes terribly fast. It isn't at all surprising to write a chapter in a day, which for me is about twenty-two pages. When it's going badly, it isn't really going badly; it's just the beginning. The first page and the first chapter are a matter of endless fiddling, cutting out all the good bits, putting in a whole lot of verbiage. Actually, it's my only way of thinking. Without a pen in my hand I can't think. And by the way, not every aspect of the monk is observed.

INTERVIEWER

What are the "good" parts you cut out? Do you keep them for further use?

LE CARRÉ

The good parts are usually the bits of gorgeous prose that stick out like sore thumbs. No, I have never made use of them later. If I fish them out of a drawer, they usually embarrass me and I chuck them away.

INTERVIEWER

Do you go from *A* to *Z* or do you bounce all over the place?

LE CARRÉ

I go from *A* to *Z*, but via a whole lot of hieroglyphics we've never met.

INTERVIEWER

What do you say to Norman Rush, who charged you with anti-Semitism in his review of *The Tailor of Panama*?

LE CARRÉ

I tell you, I have had some pretty big tomatoes thrown at me in my time, but this one missed. This one is completely nutty. For those of you who don't know—and I imagine the whole of New York knows—I am a red-toothed anti-Semite. And the reason for this, according to today's *Times*, is that my beloved Harry Pendel, who is the very heart of the story, is described by the writer of this piece as a Jew. Now, you and I know perfectly well that in Jewish law a Jew has to have a Jewish mum. Harry Pendel's mum was an Irish Catholic. That's our first problem. However, I made Harry Pendel a mixture of different traditions, as I myself am a mixture of different traditions—son of a criminal, working-class kid, sent to a smart school, learned to speak proper. He was my cocktail. He was the equivalent of me in literary terms. I am told by today's Sunday *Times* that he is a Judas Iscariot avatar. Now Hindus in the audience may be distressed by this misuse of *avatar*, and I hope that political correctness will assert itself, and that the gentleman will apologize to Hindus for misusing these religious symbols. I can only say that it simply isn't me; he's writing about a mirage, he's writing about something in his own head. All my life, ever since I started writing, because of the extraordinary childhood I had — the early introduction to the refugee problem in central Europe and what not — I have been fascinated, enchanted, drawn to and horrified by the plight of middle European Jews. It has infected my writing — book number one, book number three, *The Spy Who Came in from the Cold*, I could go on. It is the one issue in my own life on which I may say I have a clean record. I just want to say that. And if I blame anyone, it is only *The New York Times*. All writers write dotty stuff; I do the same. The editor should have said, "This guy's gone off the reservation." If there's anybody here connected with that paper, I hope they'll go back and, I don't know, light a fire or something.

INTERVIEWER

In every book of yours there seems to be a division between the first hundred pages and the rest of the story, which tends to be much clearer than the initial section. Why is that?

LE CARRÉ

I have bad habits, like we all do, and one of them is to spend much too much time on the first hundred pages of a book. I always think that if I had another life, I would write the first hundred pages and then start again. It's a principle of mine to come into the story as late as possible, and to tell it as fast as you can. The later you join the story, the more quickly you draw the audience into the middle. But beginning late requires a lot of retrospective stuff, and that's a problem I think I will always be dealing with.

INTERVIEWER

Your characters always seem to be searching for their own identities.

LE CARRÉ

Yes, that's true, but it's part of the golden center that one can never touch. I'm looking for mine, they're looking for theirs.

INTERVIEWER

Do you set out intending to say something about morality?

LE CARRÉ

No, it isn't as altruistic as that. I think it's the unconscious, irreconcilable fact inside one's own self, feeling a very flawed person and really making a search through the possibilities of one's own character. I think that most of my books are part of some process of self-education, often about the places I go to. Most of all, they are about the peculiar tension between institutional loyalty and loyalty to oneself; the mystery of patriotism, for a Brit of my age and generation, where it runs, how it should be defined, what it's worth and what a corrupting force it can be when misapplied. All that stuff is just in me and it comes out in the characters. I don't mean to preach, but I know I do, and I'm a very flawed person. It's quite ridiculous.

INTERVIEWER

A number of books purporting to be guides to your work have been published. What do you think of these and do you cooperate with the authors?

LE CARRÉ

I haven't read any of them. I became very embarrassed by that stuff. But of course I was very proud, as anybody would be, of creating a private world out of the real one, and of making it work in literary terms. After three BBC television series of my stuff, I began to get withdrawal symptoms about the Smiley cult and the le Carré cult. I didn't want to be that person. One way of dealing with that was simply to refuse to read the critical spin-off, and refuse to take notice of it. *The Tailor of Panama* is the first book in a long time on which I have read reviews. Usually Jane reads them. I always argue that you should not accept the value of good reviews, because if you do you have to accept the bad ones.

INTERVIEWER

What is it like to talk to an arms dealer?

LE CARRÉ

I just do my absolute best to be a fly on the wall. The most acute moment of this sort was when I went to Moscow to explore for *Our Game*. I went with the Chechen and the Ingush groups that were hanging around in Moscow. All I wanted to do, exactly as when I was with the Palestinians in south Lebanon, was listen, find out what made them tick, just listen. But I also wanted to meet a Russian mafia boss, and through a variety of contacts, mainly ex-KGB people, it was finally made possible for me at two or three in the morning to meet Dima. Dima came into the nightclub, which he owned and which was guarded by young men with Kalashnikovs and grenades strapped to their belts. He came in wearing Ray-Bans with his hookers and his men and his people. He looked like the Michelin Man, he was so blown up with steroids. The music was so loud I had to kneel down to get close enough to his ear to talk to him, so I seemed to be actually kneeling in his presence. My interpreter was kneeling beside me. Dima gave me the whole spiel about how "Russia is anarchic . . . yes, I've killed people; yes, I've done this and that . . . but actually I've done nothing against the law; it was all self-defense. Anyway, the law doesn't work for post-communist Russia." And I said, "Dima, let me ask you a question. In the United States, great crooks have with time become serious members of society. They've built museums and hospitals and stadiums. When, Dima, do you think that you might feel it was necessary to take on your responsibility for your grandchildren, your great-grandchildren?" Dima started talking and my interpreter all of a sudden fell into a dark silence. I said, "What is it, Vladimir? What's he saying?" He said, "Mr. David, I am very sorry, but he says fuck off."

INTERVIEWER

Have you ever considered writing more nonfiction, to add to the scattering of articles you have already written?

LE CARRÉ

I think that for as long as I can do the novel, and I really feel the buzz, that's what I should do. Also, the professional deformation of persistent fiction writing makes it very hard to stick to the truth. It's an awful thing to say, but I've almost ceased to be an accurate reporter, because the systems and the cogs won't stop turning. I have to get it down very quickly and stick to it, or I start embroidering in no time.

INTERVIEWER

How do you settle on an ending?

LE CARRÉ

Most of the endings are apocalyptic. I don't believe I've ever doubted endings. I play around endlessly with the beginning and the middle, but the end is always a goal. Certainly, when I saw the Berlin Wall going up—I was there to flesh out our station in Berlin—when I conceived that story, *The Spy Who Came in from the Cold*, which I wrote in five weeks, I was determined that he would be killed at the wall. They both would. *A Perfect Spy* and *The Tailor of Panama* had to be ended with a forfeit. It's the Gothic gloom that takes over in me at some point.

INTERVIEWER

Did you ever want to be an actor or write for the stage?

LE CARRÉ

I've often thought of writing for the stage. Other people always think that I should be an actor, and once, catastrophically, I appeared in one of my own films. I had about eight words to say, and we did sixteen takes. George Roy Hill kept looking at me and saying, "David, that's too broad. David, that's dull. Do it again." Either he was just torturing me or I was as bad as I think I was.

Novel writing spoils you, that's the problem. In novel writing you dress the stage, you dress your characters, you know exactly how they speak, you know in your own imagination exactly how they look. You want everybody to have a different perception of them. I think I'm forfeit for the stage, as I am for screenwriting. I simply cannot entrust the other jobs to other people. It's a strange thing, but it's so.

INTERVIEWER

How did you develop the character of Jim Prideaux in *Tinker, Tailor, Soldier, Spy?*

LE CARRÉ

Jim Prideaux was a schoolmaster who had been terribly betrayed by a man he greatly loved in the British secret services. I taught quite a lot when I was young. Before I taught at Eton I taught at a school for disadvantaged kids. During that time I met a lot of the strange underlife of Brits who go into private-school teaching. There was a very good schoolmaster at one of the schools where I taught—a big, rugged fellow with a limp. I used to think that that was the outer shell for Jim. And in that story Jim was set against a little boy who was a watcher, a little spy fellow. In fact, that child was written into my life because I was a duty master one night at this school for disadvantaged kids, and somebody came to me and said, "Please, Jameson is trying to kill himself." They took me to this stairwell in a big Victorian house, and there was a little kid standing on the banister at the top, with a marble floor forty feet below. Everyone was petrified. And I just went and scooped him up. He didn't jump. And when we were alone I said, "Why did you do that?" He said, "I just can't do the routine. I can't make my bed. I can never make it to class promptly. Everybody teases me." It was that little child in *Tinker, Tailor, Soldier, Spy* whom Jim Prideaux espoused; they make a common bond. I love people who can spot a victim, and Jim could because he was one himself.

INTERVIEWER

What is your opinion of ex-Stasi chief Markus Wolf? Did he help inspire you to create Karla?

LE CARRÉ

Markus Wolf was the head boy of East German intelligence, the branch that was charged with spying on West Germany. He was imprisoned briefly after the wall came down and Germany was unified. He was brought before a constitutional court in Karlsruhe, I think—they tried to put him inside for all the bad stuff he'd done. And one of the things that was said about Markus Wolf was that he had been the model for my character Fiedler in *The Spy Who Came in from the Cold*. Now, that is, in a word, sheer nonsense. I knew nothing of Markus Wolf when I wrote *The Spy Who Came in from the Cold*. If you want my personal opinion, it's a brand of postwar euphoria that I absolutely loathe. "Actually, your Spitfires were nearly as good as our Messerschmitts." In my view, Markus Wolf knowingly served a completely corrupt and disgusting regime, and there was no justification whatever for the methods he used. I think that Markus Wolf is the modern equivalent of Albert Speer. I think that sooner or later, instead of being a good German, he will be revealed for the nasty little twerp he was.

INTERVIEWER

Our last question. If you could construct a composite writer, what attributes would be conferred?

LE CARRÉ

I would give to a composite writer all the virtues I have not got, but the trouble is, I am not sure he would be able to write. I would give him clarity of vision, independence of public acclaim, the early experience of happy heterosexual love between two good parents and a voracious appetite for other people's writing. Then I would fall asleep.

—**George Plimpton**

from Burning the Days

James Salter

A Sport and a Pastime, Light Years

    In Manhattan, in the lower right-hand corner, I had found a place in which to write, a room near the river, within sight of the cathedral piers of the Brooklyn Bridge. It was on Peck Slip, a broad street near the fish market, strewn with paper and ripped wood by the time I arrived each morning, but quiet with the work of the day by then over. I wrote in this room with its bare wooden floor and ruined sills for a year—it was 1958—struggling with pages that turned bad overnight.

    I was thirty-three years old and knew no other writers. There were some artists in the neighborhood living in lofts with girlfriends or wives, and around the corner, up dank stairs smelling of urine and landings heaped with rubbish and torn mattresses, was a dedicated sculptor, Mark di Suvero. He had the entire floor. The windows were unwashed and a few bare bulbs provided light. Sculpture of ambitious scale stood here and there. In one corner, up near the metal ceiling, was a bed mounted on four tall columns. It was warmer up there, he explained, and you couldn't, if you were tired, just casually flop down. Also there was nothing devious about venery—you had to help her up, there was full complicity. Nearby was the potbellied stove, which supplied heat and on which, comrade-like, we sometimes cooked dinner, fish usually—he swept the store downstairs in return for food—sautéed with onions.

I liked to talk to di Suvero. I was certain of his authenticity, probably because I felt I had none myself. I was from the suburbs; I had a wife, children, the entire manifest. Even in the city I found it hard to believe I was working on anything of interest. Di Suvero was the opposite. Unburdened and inspired he could do as he liked, see no one, work until dawn.

He had given me a book of Rilke's poems in which there was one, "Torso of an Archaic Apollo," that seemed to have been written for me to read it. The poem described, in a restrained way, a beautiful statue in what I remember as the quiet green of a park, the perfect limbs, the grace. It came within a moment of going on too long until its final surprising line, which was simply, *You must change your life.*

It was a difficult process, the changing. Only a few people offered any encouragement, even unknowingly. Kenneth Littauer was one. Littauer and Wilkinson was the firm, its name printed on the frosted-glass door. Down on the street were clothing stores and traffic. White-haired by the time I knew him, a former editor like his partner, Littauer knew France well. He spoke French perfectly, at least inside the door of the St.-Denis, a small restaurant in the East Fifties that he favored, where, teeth blackened from his pipe, he chatted in slang with the headwaiter. He wanted to *se débarbouiller*, he said, to wash up. "*Oui, mon colonel.*"

"If this book isn't accepted . . ." he said, to help prepare me for the possibility.

"I'll start another."

I felt he expected me to say it. He was a man of integrity, diligent and pessimistic. Max Wilkinson, in contrast, was a sport. Small finger extended, he would stroke his nose during conversation in a characteristic gesture of disbelief and thought. He dressed well, blazer, pearl-gray slacks. He was interested in shares, wealth, unconventional men, scoundrels.

There was something surrendered about him, the ghost of an earlier, finer world. His people had come here in 1623, he remarked carelessly. Doomed gallantry, vain hopes, it seemed to imply. He liked to tell of going, when he was a magazine editor, to see Scott Fitzgerald. "I had a manuscript of his that I wanted to sit and go over with him. When we arrived he was drinking a water glass full of gin."

We were at the Century Club or Toots Shor's, the drinks beginning to have an effect. Fitzgerald, he said, had disappeared that night, gone upstairs and then come down again, completely naked, saying, "I know what you really want. You want to see me take my dope. Well, I'll show you."

I was inclined to believe his stories, which were seldom repeated. They were like accidental memories.

Of the years that followed, the 1960s, I remember the intensity of family life, its boundlessness. It was an art of its own—costume parties; daring voyages in an old sailboat, a leaky Comet, far out on the river; dogs; dinners; poker on Christmas night; ice skating. We were in a world of families, all young, unscarred: the beautiful Dutch girl and her husband; the painter and his wife who unexpectedly opened a restaurant on the highway, named for one of his heroes, del Piombo; the psychiatrist and his wife who were our first close friends. It was all an innocent roundelay, a party of touching originality being carried on in the midst of real-estate transactions and countryside that was slowly falling, field by field, to builders.

We lived, for the most part, in a half-converted barn near New City, about thirty miles from New York. Of all the houses this remains the clearest—the cozy room that was made into a study just off the front door, the long bright bathroom with a row of windows above the sink looking down on trees and a shed that served as garage, the stone fireplace, the rough wood floors, the huge kitchen. There was a terrace of large squares of slate that had once served as sidewalk in Nyack, and in back, through woods, was a stream. Still farther one came to a long, slanted field planted each year with tomatoes, the mere gleaning of which was a harvest. Fingernails black with earth, we brought basketfuls back to the house in the fall.

Not far away, on South Mountain Road, was the aristocracy. The early artists had settled there, and Maxwell Anderson, the playwright, had owned a house designed by Henry Varnum Poor. Of the latter I knew only that his name was attached to certain structures like a particle. The one I was most familiar with had blue walls and rooms of inherited art, Bonnards and Utrillos, Vuillards and Cézannes. "Callas just left," they might have said.

The seasons passed in majesty: summer's inescapable heat, the storms of winter, the leaves of autumn, which in a single night fell from the elms along the road. A few days later I drove through. In the great arcade a wave of yellow leaves was rising, driven into the air again by wind, as far as one could see. It was, unknown to me, a foretelling of what was to come, the time still far off when the beautiful debris would rise again and I would write about those days.

The famous figures, writers who taught at universities and were nominated for awards, were still lofty to me and remote from the path I was beating between country and town, diurnal in, nocturnal out, listening to the car radio and watching the black, familiar road unreel before me.

I had written a third book, some of it during a summer in Colorado, some in the Village, fragments of it scribbled on the empty passenger seat while driving to one place or another reciting to myself, rehearsing. It was not a maiden book. It was the book born in France in 1961 and 1962. I had a letter from Paula, the girl in that book, written at that time that urged, *the important thing, and I go back to what we used to talk about when we were twenty-one and twenty-two, is to do the things you believe you can do, and want to do and will do.*

It was my ambition to write something—I had stumbled across the words—*lúbrica y pura*, licentious yet pure, an immaculate book filled with images of an unchaste world more desirable than our own, a book that would cling to one and could not be brushed away. During its writing I felt great assurance. Everything came out as I imagined. The title was partly ironic, *A Sport and a Pastime*, a phrase from the Koran that expressed what the life of this world was meant to be as against the greater life to come.

I was at the time under the spell of books which were brief but every page of which was exalted, Faulkner's *The Sound and the Fury* or *As I Lay Dying*. This sort of book, like those of Flannery O'Connor, Marguerite Duras, Camus, remains my favorite. It is like the middle distances for a runner. The pace is unforgiving and must be kept up to the end. The Finns were once renowned for running these distances and the quality that was demanded was *sisu*, courage and endurance. For me the shorter novels show it best.

This almost perfect, so I believed, book was turned down by my publisher out of hand. Other publishers followed suit. The book was repetitive. Its characters were unsympathetic. Perhaps I was mistaken and in isolation had lost my bearings or failed to draw the line, emerging as a kind of hermit with skewed ideas. At last the manuscript was brought to the attention of *The Paris Review*, which had a small publishing capability, and it at once agreed to take it.

That year, in the autumn evening I hurried towards corner newsstands, their light spilling on stacks of papers, to pick up the just arrived issue of *The New Yorker*, which was running, in four long parts, the entire book that turned its author, Truman Capote, from a kind of pet into a blazing celebrity.

In Cold Blood filled me with envy for its exceptional clarity and power, and my admiration was all the greater since I remembered the original chilling article in the *Times*, the prosperous farm family brutally executed in their own home in safe, rural Kansas. I had even cut it out of the paper, it seemed so monstrous and foretelling. Capote, to his great credit, had done more. In a terrific gamble he had set out, flagrantly daring and astute, with nothing besides his talent and a notebook, to lay bare every facet of the crime he could discover. It was a gamble because the case might never be solved and all his time and energy might be wasted. As it was, the murderers were for a long time uncaught.

Blood, sex, war and names—the same bouquet goes for the *Iliad* and the front page. *In Cold Blood* was somewhere between the two, an enormous success. Capote soared to the heights. He was clever, his tongue wickedly sharp. He had already swooped through the bright lights developing the diva persona that was to prove irresistible, and now there was money, too.

That November he gave a great party, a masked ball, at the Plaza. The guests, in the hundreds—the list of those invited had been kept secret—were a certain cream. Many came from prearranged dinners all over town, movie stars, artists, songwriters, tycoons, Princess Pignatelli, John O'Hara, Averell Harriman, political insiders, queens of fashion, women in white gowns, men in dinner jackets. They were going up the carpeted steps of the hotel entrance, great languid flags overhead, limousines in dark ranks. The path of glory: satin gowns raised a few inches as they went up on silvery heels. Stunning women, bare shoulders, the rapt crowd.

They woke, these people, above a park immense and calm in the morning, the reservoir a mirror, the buildings to the east in shadow with the sun behind them, the rivers shining, the bridges lightly sketched. There were no curtains. This high up there was no one to see in.

In the small convertible I had bought in Rome I was driving past that night and for a few moments saw it. I knew neither the guests nor the host. I had the elation of not being part of it, of scorning it, on my way like a fox to another sort of life. There came to me something a nurse had once told me, that at Pearl Harbor casualties had been brought in wearing tuxedos, it was Saturday night on Oahu, it was Sunday. The dancing at the club was over. The dawn of the war.

In the darkness the soft hum of the tires on the empty road was like a cooling hand. The city had sunk to mere glowing sky. My own book was not yet published, but would be. It had no dimensions, no limit to the heights it might reach. It was deep in my pocket, like an inheritance.

———

In January 1972, on smooth blank pages and in hours of undisturbed solitude I began another book. I was nervous and elated. I knew what I wanted: to summarize certain attitudes towards life, among them that marriage lasted too long. I was perhaps thinking of my own. I had in mind a casting back, a final rich confession, as it were. There was a line of Jean Renoir's that struck me: The only things that are important in life are those you remember. That was to be the key. It was to be a book of pure recall. Everything in the voice of the writer, in his way of telling. I had a list of sufficiently inspiring titles, *Nyala, Mohenjodaro, Estuarial Lives*. I was writing to fit them, though in the end none survived.

This was in Colorado, in Aspen when it was only a remote town. Behind the old wooden house with its linoleum floors was a building that had been a garage and was now a studio with blue, stenciled boards high up on the ceiling, a fireplace and a counterlike desk along the wall. Writing is filled with uncertainty and much of what one does turns out bad, but this time, very early there was a startling glimpse, like that of a body beneath the water, pale, terrifying, the glimpse that says: it is there.

In the spring, confident, I sent the first seventy-five pages of what I had written off to publishers. Absolutely must have it, I imagined them saying. The replies, however, were at best equivocal. Farrar, Straus turned it down. Scribner's. As rejections came, one by one, I was stunned. I lay in bed at night wrapped in bitterness, like a prisoner whose appeal has failed. I tried to think of the books that amounted to something only after having begged, so to speak, at many doors.

Finally, a well-known editor whom I had met once or twice agreed to take the book. This was Joe Fox.

He was then in his late forties — Harvard (swimming-team captain), divorced (man-about-town), backgammon player, also squash, and acquainted with almost everyone. He was a Philadelphian, though he had lived in New York for years among, with other things, irreplaceable pieces of furniture that had been in the family since Colonial times. He had the prep-school habit of referring to himself by his last name. "Fox here," he would announce on the phone when he called. I do not mean to say he was snobbish or Anglo, however. He did have his systems and rules and was eligible for any club, but he was also supremely democratic and loyal, a man who did his work in a shirt and tie, the work that God and class, not to mention the publishing house, expected. He liked travel, the ballet and, without the appearance of it, parties. He was somewhat deaf to argument. He lived on the south side of the park in a luxurious building that had originally been painters' studios. His apartment was lofty with a curved, white balcony above the main room and bookcases everywhere. He was the ultimate New Yorker. In the city he invariably wore a suit. He had worked first for Alfred Knopf, the legendary publisher, and was related by marriage to the Canfields and Burdens. His best friends, in all likelihood, were women, to whom he attached himself with little difficulty.

Dinners with him at Caravelle, Remi, Petite Marmite, smoked salmon in slender coral sheets, creamed cucumbers, lamb, expensive Pauillac. Dinners at a hotel in the country, a table in the bar. Winter night, black as ice. The warmth of the room, a fire burning. The Japanese woman hostess, the bartender in vest and white shirtsleeves. Mussels *à la barque*. Bacala. Women taking off their coats at the door and being shown with their escorts to tables.

The fragrant smoke rose from his after-dinner cigarette. He told of famous parties, the one of George Weidenfeld's in London. The invitation in beautiful calligraphy said *Exotic dress*. Weidenfeld himself came as a pasha. There were three orchestras, one of them on the stairs, and the most beautiful women Fox had ever seen. Couples would disappear into the garden or splendid upper floors and return after long intervals. There was that English phenomenon, an upper-class wanton who, though dropped from the guest list, came anyway. As an act of disdain she pleasured nine of the guests, one after another, in a bedroom. Marie Antoinettes and Japanese samurai lay collapsed on the sofas at dawn.

Through him one met many writers. He was like an old courtier who understood and could arrange almost anything. His nostrils were large, sometimes with hair in them. He hadn't gone to his twenty-fifth reunion at Harvard, he told me. He'd looked over the list very carefully. There were fifteen hundred names, only forty he knew, twenty-five of whom he didn't want to see again, ten, for a few minutes, and only five he liked. The figures were probably inaccurate but they were stamped with his self-confidence; his ancestors preceded Benjamin Franklin. One of them contemptuously shook Andrew Jackson's hand with his own wrapped in his coattail. At Random House his position was secure. He was not one of the razors. He was protected by his ability and by not having an ambition to run things.

The book was ultimately called *Light Years*. I remember his final comment when the editing had been completed—the manuscript had blue pencil, his, in one margin and red, the copy editor's, in the other—"An absolutely marvelous book in every way," he said, adding, "probably." I had the exultation of believing it. I wanted praise, of course, widespread praise, and it seemed somehow that Fox might assure it—he had been the editor for many admired writers, Paul Bowles, Capote, Ralph Ellison, Roth. I wanted glory. I had seen, at the Met, Nureyev and Fonteyn in their farewell performance, one of many, of *Swan Lake*—magnificent, inspired, the entire audience on its feet and wildly applauding for three-quarters of an hour after the curtain as the deities appeared, together, then one or the other, then again the two, on and on, bow after bow in weary happiness as armfuls of roses were brought to the stage.

Such tremendous waves did not fall upon writers. On Victor Hugo, perhaps, or Neruda—I could think of no others—not poor Joyce, or Pushkin, or Dante or Kawabata. For them a banquet or award or something on the scale of the scene in the restaurant at midnight when the star is preparing to leave and stands before the mirror near the bar, drawing tight the belt of his trenchcoat, watched by enthralled waiters.

When was I happiest, the happiest in my life? Difficult to say. Skipping the obvious, perhaps setting off on a journey, or returning from one. In my thirties, probably, and at scattered other times, among them the weightless days before a book was published and occasionally when writing it. It is only in books that one finds perfection, only in books that it cannot be spoiled. Art, in a sense, is life brought to a standstill, rescued from time. The secret of making it is simple: discard everything that is good enough.

The years have their closure. Many of the people upon whom I had based characters passed from sight. It was only in part an accident. They had been consumed, my interest had waned. There were exceptions. The girl of *A Sport and a Pastime* I was always curious to see again, what had become of her, the details of her life, the closet in which her dresses hung, the drawer with her folded things, the bottles of perfume, shoes. I wanted again to lie there watching her prepare as if she were alone in the room, before the performance, as it were, putting on makeup, slipping into heels. She would be twenty-eight, thirty, completely changed. In fact she was married and living in Los Angeles. There were children. It was very like the book.

I had met her at Kennedy when she first arrived in America. She came through the crowd, innocent in her beauty, filled with joy. She was eighteen. Counts had coveted her. I met her also in dreams. I went through someone's empty room and knocked at her door. "Yes, come in," she said without asking who it was; I sensed she was expecting someone else. She looked up. Everything about her. I pulled up her dress in a single motion. The incredible nakedness. Laughing, she pushed it back down. In the dream I had lost the photograph of her, I didn't have an address. "You say you adore, but I think it's something else you like," she said. She was curled up, wearing nothing. At the end of a crowded road under gray clouds my ship was preparing to sail. There was traffic, the imminence of departure. My heart was sick.

Nedra, the stylish woman of *Light Years*, I sometimes saw again, usually in the city, the last time in the house she now lived in alone — true to the book, she and her husband had eventually divorced. I loved her, her frankness and charm, the extravagance and devotion to her children. I never tired of seeing her and listening to her talk. She smoked, drank, laughed raucously. There was no caution in her.

Her old lover, one of them, sat with us that last night. Nedra had aged. The years had seized and shaken her as a cat shakes a mouse. Her jawline was no longer pure and there were small pouches beneath her eyes. Her nose had gotten larger. Her still-long hair had traces of gray. In her face, which I loved, was my own mortality. The lines at the corners of my mouth, which were more terrible than an illness — I jumped up to look each morning; they were there.

She was going to give him her father's old tie pin, she said impulsively, it was the best thing her father had owned. "Do you still have the pearl cuff links?" she asked, pulling up the sleeve of his jacket. "No. They're on the other shirt," she guessed. He lived in a small house behind hers. I had no idea if they were still intimate — she was capable of every appearance of it without the thing itself.

Hers was a singular life. It had no achievements other than itself. It declared, in its own way, that there are things that matter and these are the things one must do. Life is energy, it proclaimed, life is desire. You are not meant to understand everything but to live and do certain things. Despite all I had written about her, there was more, and the carnal scenes, a minor element, I imagined entirely. It would have been gratifying to know if they were appropriate. Some things, however, she did not talk about.

She is gone, and the other wives, too, it seems, the ones men had; they are widowed or divorced, wise from intimacy, strong-voiced. The families, like old temple columns, are broken, never to be restored. When the world was young it seemed impossible. The unions were too firm, the comfort of an open, loving heart too great. I stood on deck one winter morning, coming back from Europe by boat, near to docking, the unawakened city in gray light. A family came to the rail nearby. They were German; they'd been in first class. The woman's face was beautiful, that clarity, composure and breeding that make one long for one more chance at life. I felt a burning, terrible shame. Everything I valued was suddenly made worthless and I was plunged into confusion, trying to imagine what this marvelous woman said, how she argued, sat down at the table, slept, dressed. I could not picture a single detail of her life. I was like a desperate young boy, kept from, not even knowing that the test of elegance was close inspection, and that to her husband she was quite a different person than she was to me.

"Moritz!" she called to her child. He was as handsome, with a white hat made of crudely sewn leather and square earflaps. He was seven or eight, well-mannered. He came and stood by her, near her side. Suddenly the concept of virtue as strength was real.

I often came across her opposite, the heroine of all our books and films, still young, divorced. In a bar she was wearing a kind of toque made from a colorful scarf, tight jeans, a turtleneck shirt. How had she been, I asked.

"Hello! I'm fine. I'm settling down."

Though she was still broke, as she said. She was the daughter of a writer I knew who had reversed the usual sequence—he had published some novels first and then came the list of other roles: restaurant owner, bandleader, policeman. His daughter had been working as a waitress; she had her father's unorthodox spirit. She was going to get another job when her complexion cleared up, she said. "It's hard being alone. Will you buy me a drink?"

In fact, she hadn't been alone. She'd had a guy for a month, very straight, she explained, but nice, Notre Dame, all that. He left. "He said I was taking up too much of his time. I wanted him to move in, but he didn't love my children enough. He said he did, but he didn't. Well, you know, it's difficult. I should take the time to write down twenty lines a day, shouldn't I?" she asked.

Yes, like putting pennies in a jar, it would add up, be valuable some day, perhaps salvage her life.

That was some years ago. I don't know what became of her.

There are certain houses near the river in secluded towns, their wooden fences weathered brown. Near the door in sunlight, stiff-legged, a white cat pulls itself up in an arc. Clothes on a half-hidden line drift in the light. It is here I imagine the wives, their children long grown, at peace with life and now drawn close to the essence of it, the soft rain flattening the water, trees thick with foliage bending to the wind, flowers beneath the kitchen window, quiet days. Men are important no longer, nor can they know such tranquillity, here in perfect exile, if it can be had that way, amid nature, in the world that was bequeathed to us.

Two Poems by W.S. Merwin

Harm's Way

How did someone come at last to the word for patience
and know that it was the right word or patience

the sounds had come such a distance from the will to give
　pain
which that person kept like a word for patience

the word came on in its own time like a star
at such a distance from either pain or patience

it echoed someone in a mirror who threatened with fire
an immortal with no bounds of hatred or patience

the syllables were uttered out of the sound of fire
but in silence they become the word for patience

it is not what the hawk hangs on or the hushed fox
waits with who do not need a word for patience

passing through the sound of another's pain
it brings with it something of that pain or patience

but how did whoever first came to it convey
to anyone else that it was the word for patience

they must have arrived at other words by then
to be able to use something from pain for patience

there is no such word in the ages of the leaves
in the days of the grass there is no name for patience

many must have traveled the whole way without knowing
that what they wanted was the word for patience

it is as far from patience as William is from me
and yet known to be patience the word for patience

Clear Water

Once a child's poem began a pond of time
what followed must have flowed from what a child

remembered in time about a child
he had once been except that the poem

began in a time before the poem
and before the pond that the child remembered

once a child's pond began a remembered
time that a child followed until the pond

was the time a poem began with a pond
that a child thought he remembered once not flowing

but by the time the poem began it was flowing
once upon the memory of a child

whose poem began before he was a child
a murmur flowing from before he began

though what he remembered once began
with the poem on the pond of a child's time

a child began a poem once in a time
remembered with a pond that he had seen

flowing from a spring he had never seen
kept by an unseen giant who once was a child

whose name was Mimir before the child
began the poem once in remembered time

the giant keeps the beginning before time
in the spring of mourning under the pond of time

Michelangelo

Last Poems

1

With no less joy than grief and consternation
that You, not they, were the victim doomed to die,
the chosen souls saw great gates in the sky
swing wide—Your blood the key—for mortals here.
   Their joy: in seeing Your creature in the clear
after primal guilt and its aftermath of loss;
their grief: aghast at Your agony on the cross,
a servant of servants and true love's oblation.
   Who You were, come from where, heaven lavished clues:
all its bright eyes went dim, rock bottom split,
the mountains shuddered, and pitch-black the sea.
   He raised the elders from their glum venues,
found for lost angels a more dolorous pit.
Only man, at His font reborn, sang jubilee.

2

My eyes are saddened by so much they see,
my heart by every single thing on earth.
Except that You gave me You Yourself—Your worth,
Your kindness and Your love—what's life to me?
   My wicked ways, the allure of vanity
amid the shadows of the life I live,

O help me counter these, help and forgive!
Make this—now You've shown us You—our guarantee.

3

One way remains to loose me yet, dear Lord,
from love, that passion treacherous as inane:
make things go wrong; make weird disasters rain
on me as on Your friends; estrange the world.
   You peel of flesh the same souls You appareled
in flesh; Your blood absolves and leaves them clean
of sin, of human urges, all that's mean . . .

—translated from the Italian by John Frederick Nims

Barbara Henning

Closure & Closure

A sentence is an interval in which there is a finally forward and back. A sentence is an interval during which if there is a difficulty they will do away with it. A sentence is a part of the way when they wish to be secure.
— Gertrude Stein

The newborn fell asleep beside her mother who died in the early morning from a blood clot in her brain.
Quiet and lovely, Beth's death was a loss for millions of little girls.

Their bodies were found five miles apart in the kitchens of their homes.
The boy's mother died on a kidney machine. He died at nineteen from a virus.

He drank too much one night and then died from an overdose.
He was shot in the back. The other was stabbed and slashed repeatedly.

He passed through the door of the hotel with a little pistol in his pocket.
Both were bachelors. Both lived alone. Both were discovered at 8 A.M.

The deadly fire they started in the rafters spread to his crib.
My feathers ruffle. There's no record of his death, but he died.

Things get better, get worse and then your body is cold and stiff on a table in the mortician's room.
Your feet, once tucked into your mother's body, warm and slippery, are now hidden inside a box.

Two Poems by Bruce Bond

Narcissus

Who's to say where the man ends,
the world begins; what it is
that wakes him in a visible sweat,
a thing shored on a tide of linen,
though this much is clear: as sleep
drags its intimate figures
back into the blackened current,
a magnificent loneliness
takes its place. Then he looks up
and sees his likeness astonished

into the mirror above him,
a ghost afloat in the elated room,
flat to the ceiling and pinned there.
Who wouldn't feel uneasily blessed,
to hover that way with your bed
on your back, bearing up under
the weight of heaven, made glorious
in the ruffled wingspan of your sheets.
And with a blinding adoration
to gaze down at your own nakedness,

cast out of the living skin,
impatient to descend, jealous,
as is the way with phantoms,
of every body your body touches.
You know the sensation: as if
your flesh were the drinking glass
forever chilled and gaping.
Perhaps you see your story float

in the open hands of a book,
thinking how distant the details

where they waver, how cold
and fragile in their clarity.
You are the breath flown out
of them, hovering there,
reading softly, the way a mother
reads to a child at night.
And like the child you savor
every minute, every grief that turns
to pity, that leans to the mirror's
body to drink, becoming water.

Cruor Dei

As if we arrived through the blind extremes
of sleep, we opened our mouths, eyes closed,
and the priest laid on our tongues his coins
of bread, what we learned never to cross
with our teeth, never to rush, for at the heart
of each was God's nerve, burning and alive.

Then we washed it down with wine and Latin—
cruor dei, God's blood, the stuff I figured
flowed in everyone's body—what did I know—
though here was the glad horror of appetite
taking it in, and memories of other gods,
how they in their stories were torn apart,

exploding into the ten thousand things,
into the still conscious body of names
for things, with every word a hint of blood.
It's how I picture crowning into the world,

through the red water over rims of bone
into a little chaos of lights and gasping.

I like to think the blade binds as it cuts,
mother from child, that each solitude
ripens into a name for the other.
And as the mother looks down, her voice
is a braid of scar tissue between them.
It draws the child further into debt

he never resolves, not wholly, but sees
in the unlikely bodies of passersby,
in the man, say, caught on film, who keeps
bending back the car door, pulling a stranger
from a seat on fire—a birth of sorts,
though none is entirely his to repay.

It's only the trace, at best, a kindness
remade the way gods remake themselves
in our image, half-naked, their hands nailed
to some bare wall in sweltering Texas.
Their feet are vines crossing in the brick shade.
They would turn us all into mothers, grieving.

And among our children: debt and hunger.
Sometimes you feel them thinking, confiding
in the barely audible speech of twins.
In bad times they almost sound like hope.
Which they are. So many cuts, so many streams
of erotic letters welling up in the rift:

a lover says good-bye in the hazard lights
of an idling taxi, a pulse in the eye
she will never quite remember nor forget,
not completely, and to live just this side
of completion is to turn further inward
the way a key of light turns in a gaze.

So it is with my father in his illness,
railing at the bolted apartment door,
cursing his wife for locking up his wife.
Or swearing he is the doctor again
with patients enthralled in another room.
He is the complicated child, the latch

lifting on an intricate cage. He scissors us
into broken flocks of memory and wish
which are his own body tearing apart,
though it is tough to say he suffers
the knowledge, our sense of what he was
or will be. It could be kindness too:

the tiny dice of days stumbling through him,
the bewildering children who hold out
their shadowy bruises, too young to know
which wounds are serious — they all seem so
early on — or which ones simply clear up
with time, going clean in their own blood.

Two Poems by Barbara Goldberg

Slough of the Seven Toads

The elation of naming, that dispassionate
stance, of course it could not last. As all

first steps it was bound to lead to that first
misstep, that attenuated fall through ebony

branches into the Forest of Indifference. Oh
how to define the pain of it, the eclipse

of sky, the scales that seemed to sprout
over her eyes, the petals of love-lies-bleeding

wilting in that thicket of night? Then a headlong
plunge into the slough of the seven toads

and there defiled by false iridescence,
the barter, the intrigues, the back and forth,

that rough exchange, the petty puffery of fame,
the flat inspection of their malachite eyes.

No Small Feat

No small feat for Grief to doff
his mourning cloak, the velvet
heft of it, and its scarlet naught

emblazoned in cross-stitches, insignia
for not enough. He might easily
have kept it on, remaining wrapped

in sorrow, for surely there is enough
sorrow in this world to dwell in. If we
could earn a crown for every soul

we found shrouded in despair, why
we'd be richer than a dozen kings!
Which explains why moths grow fat,

and tailors are by nature cheerful,
day in, day out, their nimble fingers
stitching habits of our own choosing.

Three Poems by Amanda Pecor

If the Saviour Came Back to Boneville, Georgia

I watched Preacher Benson plowing his back garden with a mule
to the sprung clacking of the screen door,
and it'll sound that way when the century turns.
What returns? I wipe my mouth and
the fifties-cement-block Catfish Heaven returns
with long tubes of Wonder Bread bisecting the folding tables.
—Just by wiping my mouth like that, a gesture, like putting your finger
in the mouth of the wound in His side.
Were the red droplets blooming on the wood's small moss
ever meant for our eyes?
The bee sees a psychedelic airstrip in the mouth of the lily.
If anything can save us, it's nothing we can do for ourselves.

Because a Picture Is Worth a Thousand Words

Is this my blue portrait?
Are we living on a dark continent?
Is this my portrait against the darkening year?
I would be more convincing as a Rembrandt.
He captured the soul.
It was a hummingbird wild against the walls of the heart.

Perhaps a snapshot would be more useful.
Not some silky blur drifting from the body at death,
but stop-motion. If you could capture it on film,
the soul might look like a bumblebee in flight—
something naturally buoyant. Or maybe the bee would be
the collector of souls rather than the soul itself,

which is then the crude essence of sweetness, waiting
in the ornamental body.

All you need to make a pinhole camera is an empty shoebox.

I know a woman who believes there's a place
where nothing takes everything in, and she says,
"This is my black hole," she says,
"It is about the size of a soul,"

but actually it's a pinhole
through which light passes,
etching without volition
mechanically faithful stills
of life from her perspective:
deep fields of tulip with a distant windmill,
each enisform blade of grass,
a reposing silhouette.

Witches

Somebody takes a photo
of the little girl in a witch's suit
and it stays in the corner of a mirror
yellowing out. Ten years later
her brother goes trick-or-treating
dressed as Superman.
She lies on her bed
listening to her parents
rustle in the house below.
The soft clack of dishes
reminds her of the hag
riding a broomstick over her mother's soapy arms,
always turning on her black thread,
refusing to fly straight.

Truman Capote Meets an Idol

Dotson Rader

From Truman Capote, *an oral biography*

Truman was a great jazz buff. Peggy Lee was one of his favorite singers. So, I called up Peggy who was a friend of mine and I said, "I'm here with Truman and we'd love to take you to dinner. Are you free tomorrow?"

She said, "Yes, why don't you come for a drink around six?" Typical LA, they eat like farmers. She sends her car for us. The house is in Bel Air and it's got an enormous front door—one of these modern houses with a lot of glass and stone. There's some trouble getting the door unlocked so we stand there for a while. Then we walked in and there's the biggest living room I ever saw in my life and the longest sofa. The sofa was longer than this room. Typical Hollywood—two-floor ceilings. Peggy Lee can press a button on a console by her and the screen comes down, the projector turns on, that sort of thing. It's an enormous, dramatic, theatrical Hollywood kind of place. At one end is a solid line of glass sliding doors overlooking her gardens. Peggy is dressed in a very thin white chiffon gown. Peggy hadn't been too well; she moved slow because she had her oxygen tent with her. Truman takes one look at her and goes, "Oh, my God, I'm in the presence of an angel." He goes over to her. She doesn't move. He takes her hand, like this, kisses one finger. She says, "Can I get you something to drink?" Truman says he wants a vodka, and I say I'll have the same. She buzzes for a man to come to get us drinks. He looks sort of bewildered because she doesn't keep any liquor in the house. He brings us Perrier water. Now that irritates Truman. He wants a drink. Peggy says to him, "Well, Truman, can I show you the gardens?" So he says, "Well, all right. Show me the gardens, but then we've got to go." He really wants a drink. She goes over to the sliding glass doors and she can't get them open. So Truman says, "Let me help." So the two of them, Peggy who isn't very steady and this little guy are tugging and kicking and pulling, trying to get these doors open. And we never did get them open.

So we go to Le Restaurant, which is one of the most pretentious restaurants in America, so it's very popular in LA. It had started to pour. It came down cats and dogs. Once at Le Restaurant, Truman and I order drinks and Peggy orders a bottle of Evian water, for which I paid $50 a bottle. It came in a silver champagne holder, right? We are trying to hold a conversation in a room which has a tin roof, so you feel like you're on the western front in World War I and the Germans are machine-gunning your lines. We can barely hear a thing. Truman and Peggy and I are shouting back and forth at each other, trying to make conversation. Suddenly Peggy says to Truman, "Do you believe in reincarnation?"

Truman says, "Well, I don't know. Do you?"

She says, "Oh, yes. I've been reincarnated many times. In my other lives I've been a prostitute, princess, an Abyssinian queen . . ."

Truman sort of looks at her and says, "Well, how do you know all this?"

She says, "I can prove it. I remember being a prostitute in Jerusalem when Jesus was alive."

Truman says, "Oh really? What else do you remember?"
"Oh," she said, "I remember the crucifixion very well."
He says, "Oh?"
She says, "Yes, I'll never forget picking up the *Jerusalem Times* and seeing the headline Jesus Christ Crucified."

At that point, she gets up to go to the bathroom and Truman looks at me and says, "She's totally bonkers . . . " You've got to remember all this is shouted over the machine-gunning going on.

She comes back and they start talking about singers. Truman asks her when she got started. Then something happened that I noticed a lot with Truman . . . he would meet someone, make fun of them, although they weren't aware of it, and then they would say something that would reveal a vulnerability. Some heartache or pain, and suddenly Truman's attitude would change. One of the reasons he got along with a lot of people was that they were open with him rather than being combative. I think that's one of the reasons he hated the rich because—with the exception of a few of his closest friends like Babe—they were never open with him, they were never vulnerable around him. Unless he knew a vulnerability of yours, he never felt safe around you.

Anyway, they were talking about singers in the forties and she started talking about her mother who weighed 360 pounds and used to beat up her father all the time, and her as well. When she was eleven, her mother took a butcher knife and stabbed her in the stomach. She said she still had the scar. She started singing when she was fourteen or fifteen at this radio station in Fargo, North Dakota, and I forgot who heard her, one of the bandleaders, Jimmy or Tommy Dorsey, and brought her to Chicago to perform at the Pump Room at the Ambassador East. She arrived a couple days early with a girlfriend. They had very little money; she was scared of the town. They checked into a motel. She was so naive she didn't realize that the fleabag they had checked into was a whorehouse. She said, "All these painted girls going up and down all the time and it never dawned on me that people did that sort of thing."

When they showed up at the Ambassador East, Mr. Dorsey put them into a hotel room. For a week, until she got her first paycheck, she and her girlfriend would stay up late so that around eleven or twelve o'clock at night when people had put their room service trays outside in the hall they could go down the hall and collect buns and butter. They didn't know they could use room service.

This story touched Truman. He suddenly became very protective of her. His whole attitude changed and he asked if she could sing something. Here we are in the restaurant where the bill ended up being three hundred and some dollars for all this goddamn water. Truman and Peggy Lee sat there another thirty or forty minutes totally oblivious to everyone around them, including me, singing songs. "Bye-Bye Blackbird," "I'll Be Seeing You," and all these old standards. All the way back in the car, they talked about music and every once in a while the two of them would start singing. It was a lovely evening.

Portfolio

Bathers

Graham Nickson

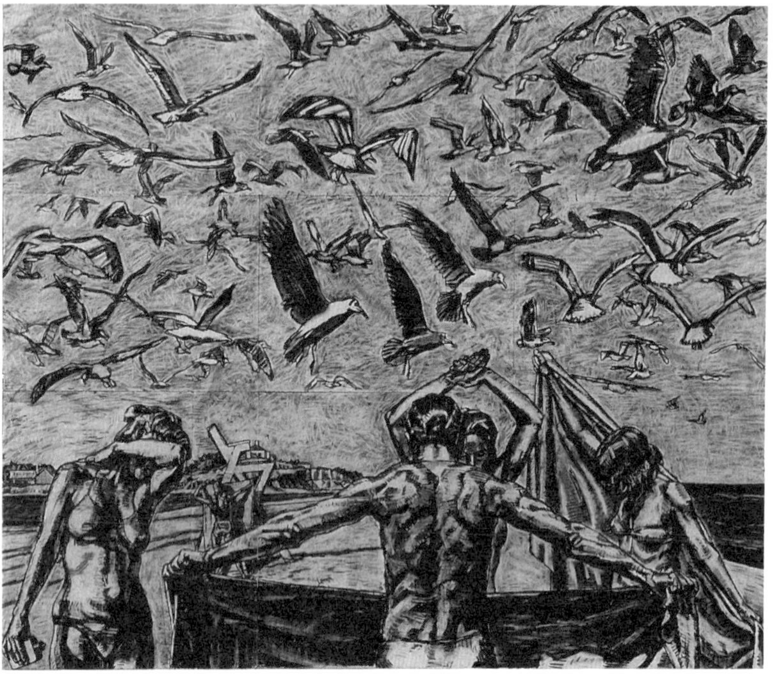

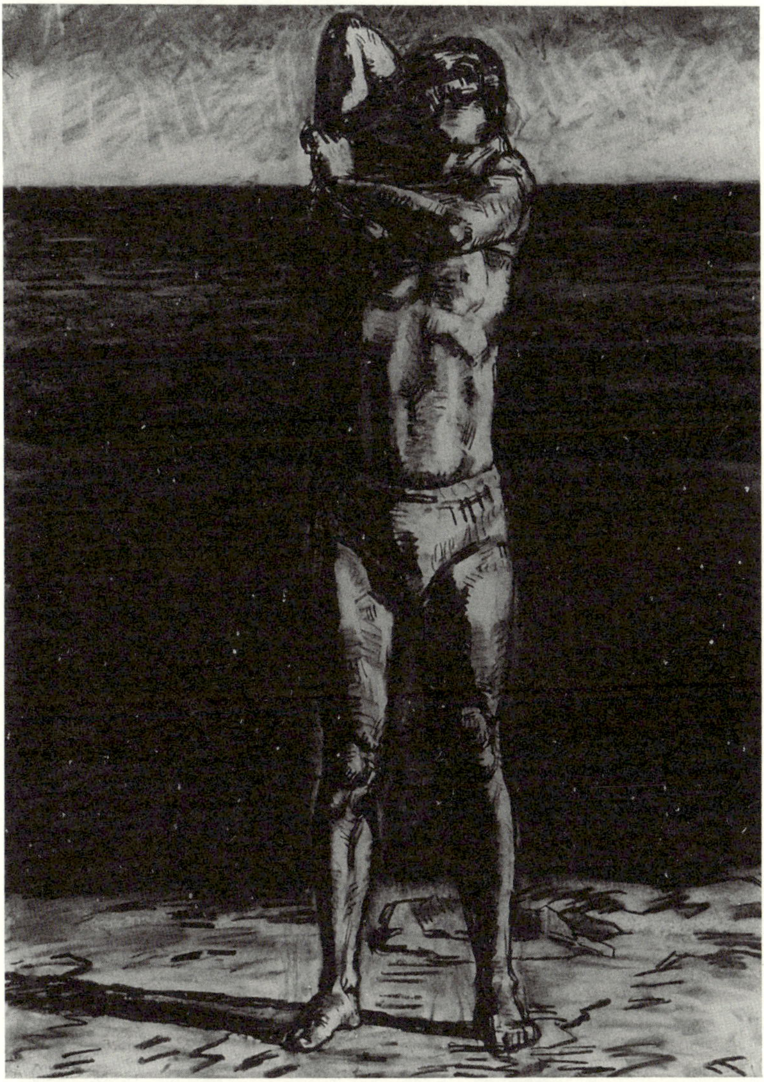

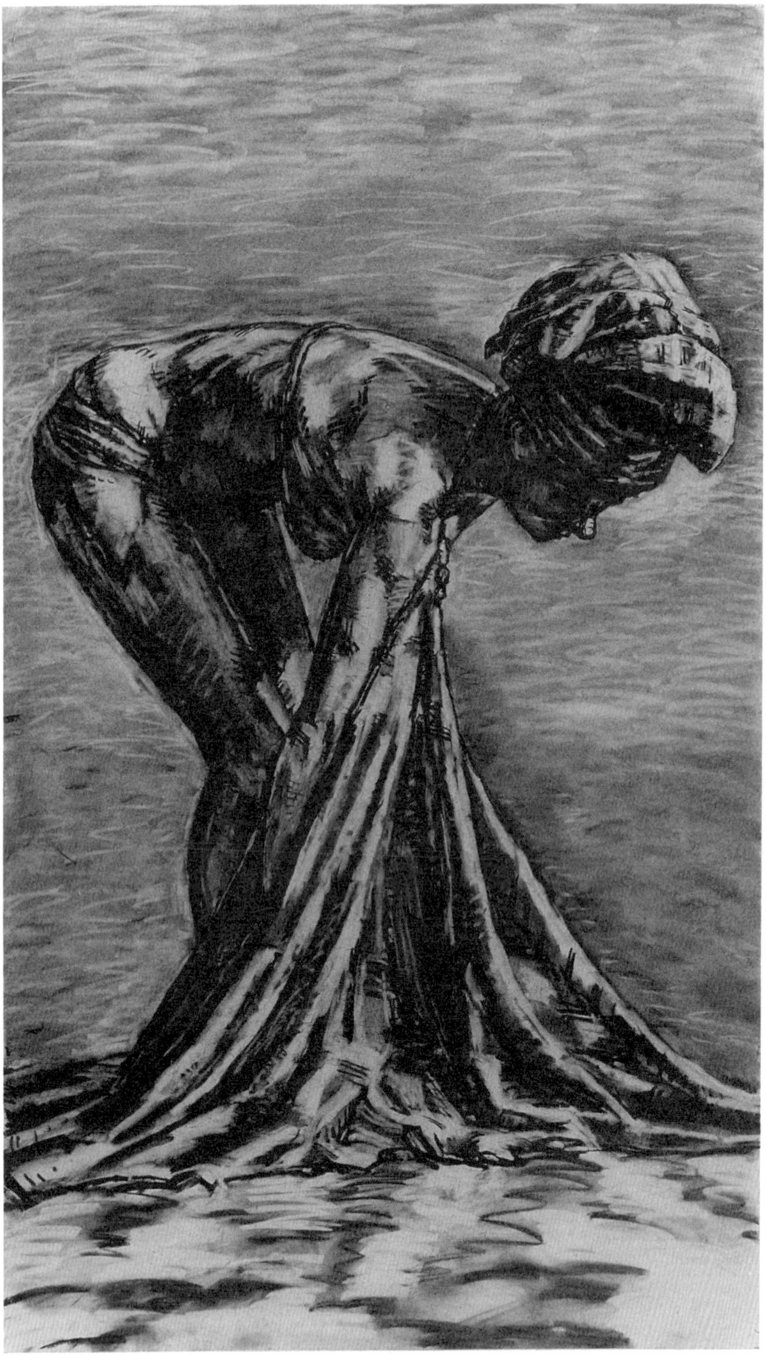

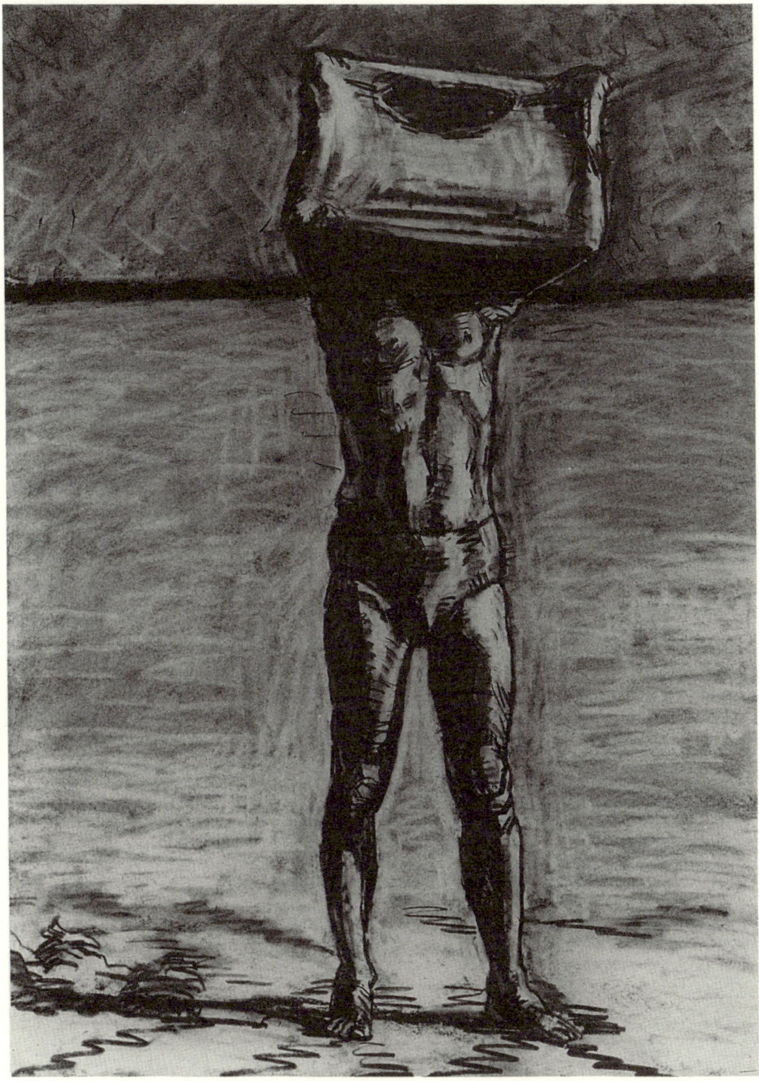

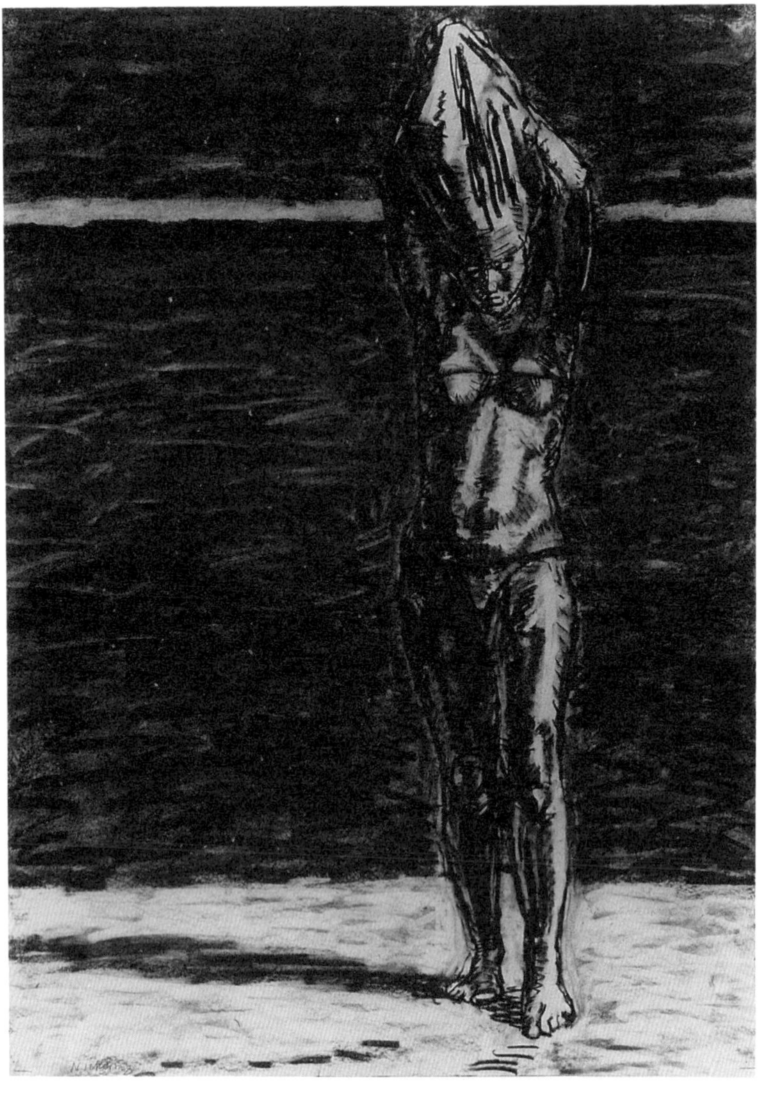

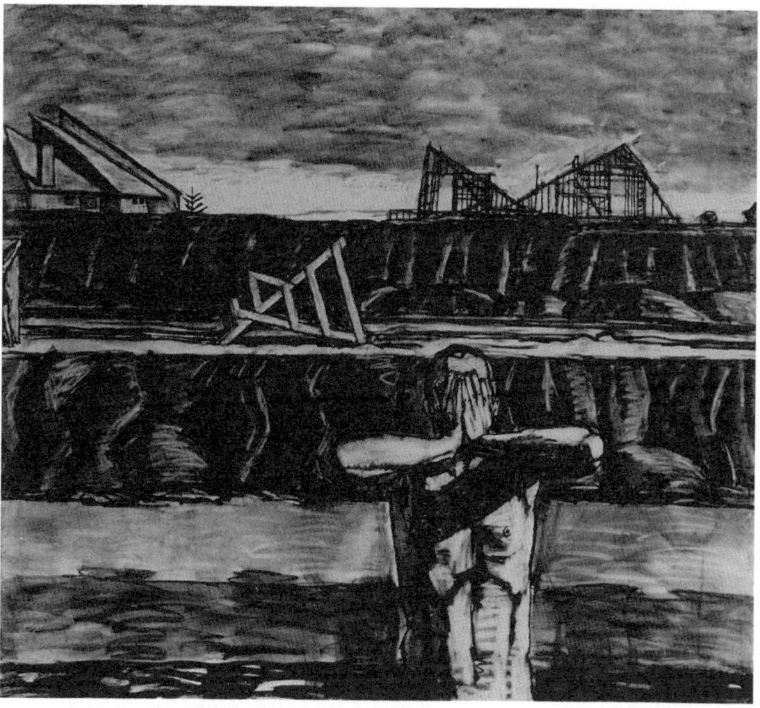

Ugly Girl

Joyce Carol Oates

I wasn't born ugly. I've seen snapshots of myself as a baby, as a toddler. Beautiful little girl with springy dark curls, shining dark eyes, a happy smile. (Possibly if the snapshots were in sharper focus you'd see imperfections.) There aren't many of these old snapshots and there's a suspicious absence of others in them—now and then adult arms positioning or lifting me, an adult in trousers seen stooping from behind (my father?), a woman's lap (my mother?). When I lived at home I'd stare at these snapshots with my name written on the backs, in pencil—they were like riddles in a foreign language. God, I wanted to tear them into shreds!

Then one day it came to me. *That beautiful little girl was your sister. She died, and when you were born they gave her your name.*

As good an explanation as any.

"Hey waitress, over here!"
"Where you been, taking a leak? More coffee."
I came to Sandy Hook, on the Jersey shore, to waitress. The place was the Sandy Hook Diner, built to resemble an

old-fashioned railroad car, glinting like tin on the outside; a counter and stools, some tables and booths crowded together on the inside. The atmosphere was breezy and casual. A little rough. I liked it, though. Among the patrons were numerous regular customers, men, friends of the owner who whistled to get the attention of waitresses, often called out their orders from where they sat. These were men who ate their food quickly and with appetite, lowering their heads toward their plates, talking and laughing with their mouths full. Such customers were not hard to please if you did as they asked. They did not notice if my wide waitressy smile was forced, pained, faked or ironic; after the first few days, they scarcely glanced at my face. My body engaged their interest, though — my heavy swinging breasts, my sturdy muscular thighs and buttocks. I weighed one hundred forty-six pounds, at five feet six. During a hot spell in September I wore loose-fitting tank tops with no bra beneath. I wore SANDY HOOK PIER Day-Glo blue T-shirts and a short denim skirt with metallic studs that glittered like rhinestones. My single pair of jeans, bleached white and thin from numerous launderings, showed the bulging curve of my ass, and the crevice of its crack, vivid as a cartoon drawing. (I knew, I'd studied the effect in a mirror.) My bare legs were fleshy, covered in fine brown hairs; I wore sandals and, as a joke, painted the nails of my stubby toes eye-catching shades of green, blue, frosty silver. Often, at rush hours, I was out of breath, my mouth moist and slack, my long snarly hair damp and clotted as seaweed at the nape of my neck. Hauling trays bearing eggs, sausage, thick hamburgers oozing blood, french fries and fried fish fillets and clattering bottles of beer, I was a conversation piece, an impersonal object over which men could exchange sly grins, roll their eyes, sniff provocatively in the area of my crotch and murmur innuendos as I set plates before them — "Mmmm baby, this looks *good*." I learned to obey, like a good-natured dog, earsplitting whistles, even to laugh at my own haste. In high school I'd been a good athlete, not a good student. I didn't mind sweating in public.

  The man who owned the Sandy Hook Diner, Lee Yardboro, a barrel-chested guy in his forties, bulldog face and bulging pale-blue eyes, sometimes liked me well enough; other times, everything I did seemed to piss him off. Once, struggling with a heavy tray, I lurched into the kitchen and Mr. Yardboro stormed in behind me and pinched the flesh of my upper arm—"Slow down, babe. You're panting like a horse." I laughed nervously, as if Mr. Yardboro had meant to be funny. His chunky teeth were bared in a grin and the clusters of broken capillaries in his cheeks gave him the look of a cheery, good-natured guy, but I knew better.

I began to notice a frequent if not regular customer in the Sandy Hook Diner. He'd signal for a waitress by raising a hand and actually lowering his head, his eyes swerving downward in a kind of embarrassment or shame. He always wore a tweed suit and a buttoned-up white shirt and no tie; he was a big, ungainly man, well above six feet, must've weighed two hundred twenty pounds, with a boyish-fattish face, and an oblong head like an exotic squash, and heavy-lidded, hooded eyes that settled upon me, or upon my body, with a look of frowning disapproval. *Ugly girl! Showing yourself like that, in public.*

This character was ugly, himself. Eye-catching ugly. But ugliness in a man doesn't matter, much. Ugliness in a woman is her life.

In fact, he reminded me of a math teacher at our junior high (my hometown was an hour's drive inland from Sandy Hook, in central New Jersey) who'd quit or been fired when I was in seventh grade; but this man seemed too young to be Mr. Cantry, I thought. That had been nine years ago.

The man in the tweed suit wore his hair clipped short, in a crew cut. It was a flat metallic color, a non-color, like his eyes. He seemed always to sit in my section of the diner, in a corner booth. There he'd read a book, or give that impression. His expression tightening as I approached with my pert waitress smile and sauntering hips, order pad and pencil in hand. There would be no small talk here. No crude-sexy banter. No laughs. I felt a physical repugnance for the man but had to admit he was always cordial, courteous. Called me "waitress" — "miss" — and left a sizable tip, as much as twenty percent, which was twice as much as most customers at the Sandy Hook. I'd call brightly after him, "Thank you, sir!" as much to embarrass him as to express gratitude, for in truth I didn't feel gratitude, I was likely to be more contemptuous of customers who tipped me well than of those who didn't.

The man in the tweed suit wasn't known by name in the diner. Behind his back, he was referred to as "Lover Boy" — "Fag Boy." The word *fag* on anyone's lips aroused particular hilarity. You'd have thought that Lee Yardboro who owned the diner would feel protective of any customer, and grateful, but that wasn't the case. When Mr. Yardboro cracked one of his jokes everyone laughed, including me, in a way I'd cultivated in high school that was laughing-not-laughing; making helpless choking sounds as if I was trying not to laugh, shoulders and breasts shaking.

Sometimes I saw the man in the tweed suit on the street in Sandy Hook, always alone. Walking with mincing steps as if his legs hurt. One day I saw him on the pier, walking slowly, staring at the ground, oblivious of the glittering ocean, the waves crashing and throwing up spray only a few yards from him. I wondered what he was thinking that was so much more important to him than where he stood. I envied him, sunk so deep in himself. As if he mattered!

I never followed the man in the tweed suit, I only observed from a distance, unseen. When I wasn't working my shifts I had a lot of time to kill. My rented room in a converted Victorian house depressed me, so I avoided it. Even as I had to admit (I'd boasted to my family) it was a bargain, at off-season rates, and only five minutes from the ocean by foot. There was a telephone for my use even if I had no one I wanted to call, and no one to call me. There was a double bed with a mattress soft as something decomposing in which, every night, for as long as ten hours if I could manage to stay asleep that long, I lay in a deep dreamless sleep like a corpse at the bottom of the ocean.

What did I look like, aged twenty-one? I wasn't sure.

Just as fat people learn not to view themselves full-length

in mirrors, so ugly people learn to avoid seeing what it's pointless to see. I wasn't what you'd call fat, and took a perverse satisfaction in contemplating my dumpy, mock-voluptuous female body in my ridiculous clothes, but I'd stopped looking at my face years before. When, for practical purposes, I couldn't avoid looking, I'd stand close to a mirror, sidelong, to examine parts, sections. An eye, a mouth. A minuscule portion of nose. I didn't wear makeup and didn't pluck my eyebrows (I'd plucked my eyebrows more or less out in high school, furious at the way they grew together over the bridge of my nose, wrongly confident they'd grow back) and there was no problem about scrubbing my face with a washcloth, brushing my teeth stooping low over the sink as I did once a day, before going to bed. My hair was no problem, I didn't need to look into a mirror to brush it, if I bothered to brush it; I could snip off ends myself with a scissors without consulting a mirror when it grew too long, snarly. Sometimes I wore a head rag for an Indian-funky look.

One advantage of *ugly*: you don't require anyone to see you the way a good-looking person does, to be real. The better-looking you are, the more dependent upon being seen and admired. The uglier, the more independent.

Another advantage of *ugly*: you don't waste time trying to look your best, you will never look your best.

What I remember of my face is a low forehead, a long nose with a bulblike tip, dark shiny eyes set too close together. Those dark thick eyebrows like an orangutan's. A mouth of no distinction but well practiced, before I entered my teens, in irony. For what is irony but the repository of hurt. And what is hurt but the repository of hope. My skin was darkish-olive like something smeared by an eraser. My pores were oily, even before puberty. In some eyes I looked "foreign" — another mode of ugly. In high school I was the heavy-faced sullen girl slouched in her desk picking at her pimply face. Some pimples were tiny as sand grains, others the size of boils, raging-red and painful. But irresistible. My fingernails sought out the myriad imperfections in my face, drawing pus, blood. Dabbing at wounds with a much-wadded filthy tissue. *A pimply face is a pimply soul. A scarred face, a scarred soul.* Even on duty at the Sandy Hook Diner, I'd be dreamily touching my face, scratching, picking. The worst of the acne was gone but scars remained. I'd do a fond inventory of them, reading my skin like braille. Like a blind person whose vision of herself is the true, the perfect vision; not the one you think you see.

• • •

One morning a friend of Mr. Yardboro's, a trucker who regularly ate breakfast at the diner, whistled to get my attention. And the man in the tweed suit sitting in a corner booth said to me, in disgust, "Why do you tolerate it?" I stared in surprise at him, that he'd actually spoken to me. He walked out of the diner, leaving half his breakfast uneaten. And no tip.

Later that morning when the diner was nearly empty, he returned to look for a glove he'd left behind. But we found no glove in the area of the booth in which he'd been sitting. He said, embarrassed, annoyed, "It isn't my business, of course. You, and this environment." I said, defensively, "Well. I work here." He said, "It's ugly to witness. I realize you need the employment. For why else. You seem not to expect better." He spoke in rapid spurts, as if he wasn't accustomed to speaking to another person face to face. He was staring grimly at me, a head taller than me, his thick, fleshy lips curled in disdain. He was a youngish-old man whose stomach and torso were most of him, swollen like a tumor.

I said, "I'm new at being a waitress. But I like it. I like it *here*. I'm grateful for the job."

It was true: I'd had several jobs in the past fifteen months.

It was true: I was grateful. I'd joked with myself that, if things didn't work out at the Sandy Hook Diner, in this going-to-seed resort town on the Jersey coast, I could always wade out into the surf.

"What is your age?"

"My age? Twenty-one."

"I think you were a student of mine? Years ago."

Mr. Cantry? He *was*?

"But I've forgotten your name."
"Xavia."
"Zavv-ya?"
"It's Romanian."

Xavia was no name I'd ever heard of. Like static, it had flown into my head.

Mr. Cantry frowned, as if suspecting I might be lying. He introduced himself as Virgil Cantry and put out his hand to shake mine. I had no choice but to take it, with a slight shiver.

After he left, I tried to remember what had happened to Mr. Cantry nine years ago. I hadn't liked him as a teacher — I hadn't liked most of my teachers. There'd been rumors, wild tales. He'd quarreled publicly with the school principal one day in the cafeteria. He'd slapped a boy. He'd yelled at boys throwing snowballs at his car. He'd been stopped for speeding — drunken driving — he'd resisted arrest and been beaten by police, handcuffed. Or he'd had a breakdown in some public place — a local store, a doctor's waiting room. Or maybe he'd gotten sick, had major surgery. He'd been hospitalized for a long time and when at last he was released, his job teaching seventh and eighth grade math was no longer waiting for him.

Next day, and the next, Mr. Cantry stayed away from the Sandy Hook Diner. I was relieved when he didn't show up.

Then one evening after my late shift, there he was, waiting for me in the doorway of a dry cleaner's up the block. Awkwardly expressing surprise at seeing me. It was raining, and he flourished a big black umbrella to hold over me — "Xavia! A coincidence."

So we walked together. Blindly, it seemed. Mr. Cantry wore a trench coat with a flared skirt, a visored cap tugged down tight on his odd-shaped head. He seemed excited, nervous. *He will lead you out into the sand dunes, he will rape and strangle you.* He asked if he might walk me home and I heard myself say in my bright waitressy voice, "Why not?"

Loneliness is like starving: you don't realize how hungry you are until you begin to eat.

"I'm no longer a teacher, if you're wondering. I'd describe myself as a private citizen. A witness." Mr. Cantry spoke soberly, never doubting I'd be interested in what he had to say. From his looming height he glanced sidelong at me, holding the umbrella over me at a gallant distance. I wore rust-red corduroy slacks with a fly front that barely fit me, they'd grown so tight, and a sweatshirt from my semester at a community college with the words POETRY POWER on the front; over this, a canvas jacket one of the other waitresses had been going to throw away. "I've been sick, but now I'm well. I'm *very well.* It's as if, in my sickness, 'Virgil Cantry' was burnt out, purified." He paused, breathing hard. He said, more intimately, "When you started waitressing at the diner, I believed I recognized you at once. But not your name—*Xavia*. Odd that I wouldn't recall such an exotic name."

"I wasn't an exotic student. I almost flunked math."

"No. You were an intelligent, serious student. Perhaps anxious. Mature for your age. You asked for extra-credit assignments in homework and they were always diligently done."

I laughed, surprised and annoyed. "That wasn't me, Mr. Cantry."

"Please call me Virgil. Yes, surely it was you."

I resented it that this man, a stranger, should claim to know more about me than I knew about myself.

Now we were on the narrower, darker street where I lived. It was not a street familiar to me. I was thinking that, sometime in seventh grade, around the time I'd begun to menstruate, my skin had started to erupt; it was possible that Virgil Cantry remembered me before that time. "You've moved away from your home, Xavia? You're living alone now?"

I wanted to say *Fuck you, that's my own business*. Instead I said nothing.

"*I* have never married," Mr. Cantry said. "Some natures, it isn't for them to marry. To sire children, in any case."

"You don't need to be married to have children, Mr. Cantry."

"Marriage is the legalization of *nature*. Nature demands

reproduction of the species. Blind instinct—that the species continues."

I couldn't argue with that. At least, this didn't seem to be a marriage proposal.

At the run-down wood-frame house in which I rented a room, Mr. Cantry seemed to have more to say, but decided against it. I hid both hands in my pockets so that he couldn't shake hands with me. From inside the musty-smelling vestibule I watched my former teacher carefully descend the porch steps and walk away slowly in the rain. On the porch with me he'd shut up the umbrella without knowing what he did, as if preparing to come inside the house; now, out in the rain, he'd forgotten to open it.

That night I had a rare dream, a hurt-fantasy. *At the Sandy Hook Diner required to serve the customers, who were men, naked. A filmy strip of cloth like a curtain wrapped around me, coming loose. My breasts were exposed, I couldn't conceal myself. My coarse-hairy groin. The men called* waitress! here! *Like you'd call a dog. But it was meant to be playful, they were just teasing. No one actually touched me. I had to come close to them to serve them their food, but no one touched me. They were eating pieces of meat, with their fingers. I saw bright blood smeared on their mouths and fingers. I saw that they were eating female parts. Breasts and genitals. Slices of pink-glistening meat, picked out of hairy skin pouches the way you'd pick oysters out of their shells. The men laughed at the look in my face. They tossed coins at me, nickels and pennies, and I stooped to pick the coins up and my face heated with blood and I felt a strong sexual sensation like the pressure of a rubber balloon being blown larger and larger about to burst* and I woke anxious and excited my heart beating so rapidly it hurt and cold, slick sweat covered my body inside my soiled flannel nightie and it was a long time before I got back to sleep. I didn't dream about Mr. Cantry at all.

By the end of November my shifts at the Sandy Hook Diner had been cut back. They were unpredictable, depending upon the availability of other waitresses (I gathered). One day I might begin at 7 A.M., the next day at 4:30 P.M.. Other days, I didn't work at all. I slept.

Since the evening he'd walked me home, I hadn't spoken with Mr. Cantry. When I worked the evening shift he'd linger over coffee as late as 10 P.M. in the hope of "escorting" me home.

Thanks I said. But I have another engagement.

I whispered fiercely to him not wanting anyone else to hear.

I was in perpetual terror of being fired from the Sandy Hook Diner and so moved in a trance of energy, high spirits and smiles. My wide, fixed smile was so deeply imprinted in my face, it was slow to fade after my shift ended; sometimes, waking in the middle of the night, I discovered that it had returned. *Waitress! waitress!* I heard myself summoned impatiently and turned to see no one, no customer, there.

At Thanksgiving I took a bus home not wanting to go home but my mother pleaded with me angrily on the phone and I knew it was a mistake but there I was, in the old house, the house of one thousand and one associations and all of them depressing, the smell of the roasting turkey sickened me, the smell of the basting grease, the smell of my mother's hair spray so I realized I wouldn't get through it within minutes after walking through the door and that afternoon we were working together in the kitchen and I said excuse me, Mom, I'll be right back and when I came back with the old photo album the palms of my hands were cold with sweat and I said, "Mom, can I ask you something?" and guardedly my mother said, for years of living with me had made her wary, "What?" and I said, "Promise you'll tell the truth, Mom?" and she says, "What is the question?" and I said again, "Promise me you'll tell the truth, Mom," and she said, annoyed, "How can I promise, until I hear the question?" and I said, "All right. Did I have a sister born before me, given my name, and did she die? That's all I want to know," and my mother stared at me as if I'd shouted filthy words right there in her kitchen, and said, "Alice, *what*?" and I repeated my question which was to me a perfectly logical question, and my mother said, "Of course you didn't have a sister who died! Where do you get your ideas?" and I said, "Here. These snapshots," and I opened the album to show her the snapshots saying, in a low, furious voice, "Don't try to tell me this is me, it isn't," and my mother said, her voice rising, "Of course she's you! That's you! Are you crazy?" and I said, "Can I believe you, Mom?" and she said, "What is this? Is this another of your jokes? Of course that's you," and I said, wiping at my eyes, "It isn't! Goddamned liar! It isn't! This is someone else, this isn't me! This is a pretty little girl and I'm ugly and *this isn't me*!" and my mother lost it then as often she did in our quarrels, lost it and began shouting at me, and slapped my face, sobbing, "You terrible, terrible girl! Why do you say such things! You break my heart! You *are* ugly! Go away, get away! We don't want you here! You don't belong here with normal people!"

So I left. Took the next bus back to Sandy Hook so it seemed, when I went to bed that night, early, hoping to sleep through twelve hours at least, that I'd never been gone.

The following Sunday evening Mr. Cantry came to my apartment house. It was the first time the buzzer to 3F had been rung in the weeks I'd been living here and the noise was loud as the buzzing of crazed wasps. I wished I hadn't known right away who it must be, but I knew.

Took my time going downstairs in my soiled POETRY POWER sweatshirt and jeans. And there was exactly who I'd expected. My ex-teacher squinting at me out of his shiny no-color eyes. He wore the trench coat with the flared skirt, he was turning his visored cap nervously in his fingers. "Xavia, good evening! I hope I'm not interrupting? Would you like to join me in a meal? — not at the Sandy Hook Diner." He paused for my response but I didn't smile, I said only that I'd already eaten, thank you. "Then to go for a walk? To have a drink? Is this a possible time? I saw you were not on duty at the usual place so I presumed to come here. Are you angry?"

I intended to say *Thank you, but I'm busy*. I heard myself

say, "I could take a walk, I guess. Why should I be angry?"

I'd been cool to Mr. Cantry in the diner, the last couple of times he'd come in. I didn't like him brooding in his corner booth watching me. Frowning-smiling like sometimes he didn't actually see *me*, God knows what he was seeing. And the day before, some guys had been teasing me the way some of the regular customers do, passing around a copy of *Hustler*, I was supposed to catch a glimpse of these photos of female crotches in stark close-up as in an anatomical text. My part was to pretend I didn't see, didn't know what it was I didn't see, my face blushing in patches. *Hey guys, I wish you wouldn't!* My embarrassed downcast eyes. My wide hips, my hubcap breasts inside a SANDY HOOK PIER T-shirt and unbuttoned sweater. *But it's okay I'm a good sport.* Not begging exactly, guys hate females who beg, like females who cry, makes them feel guilty, reminds them of their mothers. More like I was asking for their protection. And it was okay or would have been except there was Mr. Cantry looming up behind me, in his old teacher-voice and his mouth twisted in disdain, "Excuse me! Just one moment, please!" and the guys gaped up at him in astonishment not knowing what the hell was going on but I knew, I believed I knew, quickly I turned and tugged at Mr. Cantry's sleeve and led him back to his booth and whispered, "Leave me alone, goddamn you!" and he said angrily, "They are harassing you, those disgusting louts," and I said, "How do you know? How do you know what's going on?" So I got Mr. Cantry to settle down and I returned to the men and they were laughing, making remarks, I more or less pretended not to catch on, just a dumb waitress, smiling anxiously and trying to please her customers *Hey guys have a heart will you?* so finally it worked out, they left me tips in small coins scattered across the sticky tabletop. And took away *Hustler* with them. But I was pissed at Mr. Cantry for interfering and would have asked him never to come into the Sandy Hook Diner again except that wasn't my prerogative.

He was saying, "I hope you are not still upset? About yesterday?"

"Those customers are the owner's friends. I have to be nice to them."

"They are crude, vulgar. Animals—"

"And I like them, anyway."

"You like them? Such men?"

I shrugged. I laughed. "Men, boys. Boys will be boys."

"But not in my classroom."

"You don't have a classroom now."

We were excited. It was like a lovers' quarrel. I walked in quickened steps, ahead of Mr. Cantry. I believed I could feel the sharp stabbing pains in his legs, bearing the weight of his ungainly body.

We went to Woody's, a café I'd seen from the outside, admiring the winking lights, a preview of Christmas. Through an oval window in a wall of antique brick I'd often seen romantic couples by firelight, holding hands at the curving bar or at tables in the rear. Once Mr. Cantry and I were inside, seated at a table, our knees bumping awkwardly, the place seemed different. The firelight was garishly synthetic and a loud tape of teenage rock music played and replayed like a migraine. Mr. Cantry winced at the noise, but was determined to be a good sport. I ordered a vodka martini—a drink I'd never had before in my life. Vodka, I knew, had the most potent alcohol content of any available drink. Mr. Cantry ordered a club soda with a twist of lemon. Our waiter was young and bored-looking, staring at Mr. Cantry, and at me, with a pointedly neutral expression.

"A person yearns to make something of himself. Herself. A being of distinction," Mr. Cantry said, raising his voice to be heard over the din. "You must agree?"

I hadn't been following the conversation. I was trying to twist a rubber band around my ponytail, which was straggling down my back, but the rubber band was old and frayed and finally broke and I gave up. My vodka martini arrived and I took a large swallow even as Mr. Cantry lifted his glass to click against mine, saying, "Cheers!"

I said, feeling mean, "But why should a person make something of himself?—herself? Who gives a shit, frankly?"

"Xavia. You can't mean that." Mr. Cantry looked more perplexed than shocked, the way my mother used to look before she caught on to the deep vein of ugliness to which she'd given birth. "I don't think that's an honest response. I challenge that response."

I said, "Most people aren't distinctive. Most lives come to nothing. Why not accept it?"

"But it's human nature to wish to better oneself. That the inner being becomes outer. Not to sink into desolation. Not to—*give up*." He spoke with a fastidious curl of his lip.

"Haven't you given up, Mr. Cantry?"

This was a cruel taunt. I was aiming for the man's heart.

But Mr. Cantry considered the question. "Outwardly, perhaps. Inwardly, *no*."

"What's inward? The soul? The belly?"

"Xavia, you shock me. This is not truly you."

"If you look into a mirror, Mr. Cantry, do you seriously think that what you see isn't you? Who is it, then?"

"I am disinclined to mirrors," Mr. Cantry said, sniffing. He'd finished his club soda, ice and all, and was sucking at the lemon twist. "I have never taken mirrors as a measure of the soul."

I laughed. I was feeling good. The vodka martini was a subtler drink than I'd expected, and delicious. Blue jets of flame raced along my veins. "Do you think much about death, Mr. Cantry? Dying?"

At first I thought he hadn't heard, the noise in the café was so loud. Then I saw his stricken look. Almost, I regretted my question. In the flickering light I saw that his pallid skin, like what I recalled of my own, looked stitched together, improvised; as if he'd been smashed into pieces and carelessly mended. "Death, yes. Dying. Yes. I think about dying all the time." He went on to speak of his parents who were both deceased, and of a sister he'd loved who had died of leukemia at the age of eleven, and of a dog he'd brought here to Sandy Hook to live with him, a cocker spaniel who'd died in August at the age of only seven years. Since this dog's death, Mr. Cantry confessed, he'd had to face the prospect of, each morning, wondering where he would get the strength to force himself out of bed; he slept long, stuporous hours, and believed he came very close to death sometimes—"My heart stopping, you know, like a clock. The way my father died. In his sleep. Aged fifty-three." As Mr. Cantry spoke, I saw tears gathering in his eyes. His eyes seemed to me beautiful, luminous; his moist loose lips; even the glisten of his nostrils. My heart beat quickly in resistance to the emotion he was feeling, the emotion that pumped through me yet which I refused to acknowledge. A mean voice taunted *So that's why this guy has been trailing you. He's lost his only friend—a dog.*

I was fascinated by this ugly man who seemed not to know he was ugly. When rivulets of tears ran down his cheeks, and in embarrassed haste he wiped them with a cocktail napkin, I leaned back in my seat, and glanced around the crowded café, in a pose of boredom. Mr. Cantry's nose was seriously running and he blew it at length in a sequence of tissues and by the time he was finished, I was well out of my sentimental mood.

I drained my vodka martini and rose to leave. Mr. Cantry fumbled to follow close behind me, swaying like a man in a dream. He said, "Xavia, I think you must know—I am attracted to you. I realize the difference in age. In sensibility. I hope I don't offend you?"

There was a crush of people at the coatrack. We almost lost each other. Out on the sidewalk, in the freezing air, another time Mr. Cantry said, pleading, "I hope, Xavia—I don't offend you?"

Pointedly, I didn't answer. I'd thrown on my windbreaker and crammed my knit cap down tight on my head. The windbreaker was unisex and bulky and the navy blue cap made my head look peanut-small. I caught a sidelong glance at myself in a beveled mirror banked by ferns in the café window and winced even as I laughed. God, I was ugly! It was no exaggeration. Almost, such ugliness is a kind of triumph, like a basket you sink after having been fouled.

One day I overheard Maxine on the phone in the office, talking and laughing. Complaining to a friend, "That Lee! — he's so damned soft-hearted. Leaves the dirty work to *me*." She meant laying off employees. Dismissals.

A new McDonald's had opened a mile away. We never acknowledged such rivals. Even to allude to them jokingly would be to stir Mr. Yardboro's fury.

I had come to believe that Lee Yardboro, in his way, liked me. Yet he watched me closely, critically, as he watched all his help. If you were on Mr. Yardboro's payroll, he wanted to make sure you were earning your salary. His pale-blue slightly bulging eyes following me, mouth working as he sucked at a toothpick. *Speed it up, kid. But don't go barging around like a goddamn horse.* I obeyed Mr. Yardboro's wishes without his needing to speak. I never complained behind his back, bitterly like certain of the other waitresses. Never cut corners, never hid away in the lavatory cursing and weeping. My only weakness (which I tried to keep secret) was eating leftovers from customers' plates. Like most food workers, I'd developed a repugnance for food; yet I continued to eat, despite the repugnance; once I began eating, no matter the food, no matter how unappetizing, it was impossible for me to stop. The day I'd overheard Maxine on the phone, I pushed into the kitchen with a tray of plates and no one was watching so quickly I devoured the remains of a cheeseburger almost raw at its center, leaking blood, and several onion rings, and french fries soaked in catsup. In an instant I was ravenous, dazed. I started in on another platter, devouring the remains of some batter-fried perch, a foul-fishy taste even catsup couldn't disguise, and at that terrible moment Mr. Yardboro slammed through the swinging door whistling, must have seen me, my guilty frightened eyes and greasy mouth and fingers, but in a gesture of unexpected tact — or out of simple embarrassment, for there were things that embarrassed even Lee Yardboro — he continued on his way back into the office, pretending he hadn't seen.

Though at closing time saying, with a disdainful twist of his mouth, and his blue gaze raking me up and down, "Eat as much leftover-crap as you want, honey. Saves wear and tear on the garbage disposal."

After the *Hustler* incident Virgil Cantry stopped eating at the Sandy Hook Diner. He'd been asked not to patronize it any longer by Mr. Yardboro who told him that other customers had complained about him. I erased him from my thoughts like wiping down a sticky formica table.

Except. The blowy dark afternoon of Christmas Eve when we were closing early (it was a lonely time — Mr. Yardboro and his family were spending a week in Boca Raton, Florida), there came Mr. Cantry into the diner to ask if he could see me that evening. He wore a bulky black wool overcoat and his visored cap pulled down tight on his forehead. He looked tense, even grim. His eyes glared at me with yearning and reproach in about equal measure, as if I'd been the one to bar him from the Sandy Hook Diner. I wanted to snort with laughter *What? Christmas Eve, with you?* but I heard myself say, sighing, "Well. I guess. But only for a little while."

Maxine and I had decorated the diner for Christmas. It looked cheap, tacky, gaudy but I was sort of proud of it, actually. There were tinsel strips, plastic mistletoe and holly strung around the booths, there was a three-foot plastic Christmas tree with winking bubble lights, there was a clownish fat-bellied plastic Santa Claus beside the cash register whose nose lighted up (the joke in the diner was, this figure resembled our boss Mr. Yardboro). I asked Mr. Cantry what he thought of the decorations, making my question ironic, and Mr. Cantry looked around as if taking inventory, slowly. With his old teacherly sobriety. There was no one else in the diner at the moment and, seeing it through this man's eyes, I felt a wave of horror pass over me — that the Sandy Hook Diner was only this, the sum of its surfaces. Like one of those trendy hard-edged realist paintings of city scenes, neon, chrome, formica, plastic and glass and slick bright colors you stare at trying to comprehend why anybody's asshole enough to have painted it.

Mr. Cantry said, meaning to be kind, "It does capture a kind of Christmas spirit."

Despite his legs that pained him, Mr. Cantry insisted upon coming to get me, at my apartment, to escort me to his. Walking with him, I wondered if varicose veins raddled his legs; if his legs were pulpy-white. I wondered if his feet swelled, like mine, like twin goiters requiring soakings in Epsom salts. I wondered if his penis hung down from his fatty groin like slick blood sausage or if it was withered-looking, wizened, like a certain kind of Italian sausage.

Mr. Cantry's apartment was in a stucco apartment building with the date 1929 prominent on its portico, on a street parallel with my street, a few blocks away. It was an old, stately place, with an ornamental foyer and high ceilings. Mr. Cantry's living room had a fireplace (unused) and was crowded with old, inherited furniture. Embedded in a grimy Oriental rug as if woven into the fabric were strands of curly coppery dog hairs, and there were more dog hairs on the sofa on which Mr. Cantry invited me to sit. Heavy brocade draperies had been pulled across the windows, though not completely. There was a pervasive odor of something astringent and medicinal. A voice teased *The scene of the seduction!* While Mr. Cantry fussed in the kitchen, I examined a table laden with numerous framed photographs of Mr. Cantry's kin, heavyset, earnest persons, most of them middle-aged or elderly, in the clothes and hairstyles of another era. In front of the photographs were bright color snapshots of a cocker spaniel with butterscotch fur and watery eyes. Mr. Cantry entered the room humming, carrying a silver tray with a tall champagne bottle and two crystal goblets and a platter of sizzling sausages and cheesebits. He said, "Ah, Xavia. Monuments to my beloved dead. It should not dampen our spirits, though. On Christmas Eve."

He set the tray down in front of me as if I were a tableful of people. His eyes were moist with effort and his fingers trembled. Though I felt slightly sickened from the medicinal odor and an underlying smell of dust, dirt, grime, loneliness, I began to eat hungrily. Mr. Cantry said, "When you are the last of your bloodline, Xavia, as I am—you look backward, not forward. With children, you would of course be tugged forward. Your attentions, your hopes, I mean. Even your fears. But—forward. Into the future."

I smiled, eating. "Well, I'm not in the mood for having a baby. Even if it's Christmas Eve."

"Xavia, you say such things!"

Mr. Cantry blushed, but with pleasure, as if I'd leaned over suddenly and tickled him. I'd become the brash smart-aleck student some teachers inexplicably court. "I was not speaking of either of us—of course," he said quickly. "But only in theory." He sat on the sofa beside me, unnervingly close; he seemed to have gained, in the privacy of his apartment, a degree of masculine confidence. With some effort he uncorked the champagne—it was a French champagne with a black label and pretentious gilt script—and poured brimming glasses for both of us. He laughed as some of the bubbly liquid spilled onto my fingers and corduroy slacks. "To the holiday season, Xavia! And to the New Year which I hope will bring us—both—much happiness." There was something reckless in the way he smiled, and clicked his glass against mine, and drank. I asked, on a hunch, "Are you supposed to drink, Mr. Cantry?" and he said, hurt, "Christmas Eve is a special occasion, I think."

If you're an alcoholic there's no occasion that can be special, I thought. I'd had a drinking problem myself, not too long ago. But I kept all this to myself.

Within a half-hour, Mr. Cantry and I had drained two large goblets of champagne. We'd devoured most of the greasy sausages and cheesebits. Mr. Cantry was giving me a complicated account of his sources of income; among them was a "disability pension" from the state of New Jersey. He said, "I have never married for the very good reason that I have never yet been in love." He belched softly. There was a fizzing sensation in my head like minuscule popping bubbles, or brain cells. Transfixed, I saw a man's large hand reach for my own hand, like one hairless creature capturing another. I knew it was funny, but I was beginning to feel panic. Mr. Cantry was breathing quickly, staring at me, murmuring, "You are so mysterious, Xavia! So exotic." I said, "Do I look foreign?" He said, enunciating the word as if it were an aphrodisiac,

"'Ex-o-*tic*.'" I said, "'Ug-*ly*.'" He said, gripping my hand tighter, "*No!* Not at all. Unlike these other young women waitresses I have observed in Sandy Hook, you, Xavia, are special." I didn't like to be told that there'd been other waitresses in Mr. Cantry's life. "Yeah? Why am I so special?" I asked ironically. Mr. Cantry's fingers were locked around mine and both our hands were resting heavily on my knee. He said, "Because you were my student, Xavia. None of these others can be so close." I laughed, disappointed. I extracted my sweating hand from his and my champagne glass overturned and spilled what remained of its contents onto the sofa. "Oh, oh!" Mr. Cantry fussed with napkins, distressed. I said, "I'm going now, Mr. Cantry. I don't feel well."

This wasn't what Mr. Cantry wanted to hear. He said, breathing harshly, "You could lie down! Here, or in the other room. This is meant to be a happy occasion." I said, "I don't think I want to lie down." I stood, and the room spun. Mr. Cantry lurched to his feet to steady me but he was unsteady himself, lost his balance, and we fell to the floor in a clumsy heap. I was laughing. I was on the verge of hyperventilating. A voice teased *The scene of the rape! Strangulation!* I was crawling on my hands and knees, trying to escape. It passed through my mind that I hadn't crawled on any floor for almost twenty years, I'd forgotten how. Somehow a lamp became unplugged, this end of the living room was darkened. Mr. Cantry was on his knees beside me, panting like a large overheated dog, stroking my hair. "Xavia, please forgive me! I did not mean to upset you." I pushed at his hand in a way that might be construed as playful; the way Lee Yardboro and certain of his buddies bounced boyish punches off one another's upper arms. But Mr. Cantry was strong, and he was heavy. Now stroking my back and kissing the nape of my neck through my tangled hair, his mouth damp and yearning. "I would love you, Xavia. You are in need of strong, devoted guidance. In that place, you demean yourself. If you are punished long enough, you become guilty. This is a fact I know. Xavia—" I panicked and shoved him, hard. He fell against a table, a cascade of framed photographs crashed to the floor and their glass shattered.

I crawled away, jumped up and grabbed for my windbreaker. Mr. Cantry was calling after me, "What have you done! How could you! Please! Come back!" Blindly I ran out of the apartment and down a flight of stairs and when I got back to my own place and bolted the door I saw that it was only 8:20 P.M. of Christmas Eve. It had seemed so much later.

All the night I thought Virgil Cantry might follow me, ring the buzzer downstairs wanting to apologize. But he didn't. The phone didn't ring. I wasn't expecting my mother to call to wish me a happy Christmas just as I hadn't planned on calling her, either, and this turned out to be true.

• • •

Two days later when I went in to work at the Sandy Hook Diner, I learned that Virgil Cantry had been arrested on Christmas Day for prowling in backyards and trying to look in a woman's windows. Gleeful Maxine showed me the Sandy Hook *Gazette*, a brief paragraph in the police blotter column and a blurred photo of a man shrinking from the camera, trying to shield his face in a classic pose of shame. "That's him, isn't it? That guy who used to come in here all the time?" I took the paper from Maxine and read, amazed that on Christmas Eve a local woman had reported a male prowler in her backyard, a man peering into her windows; she'd screamed, and he'd run away, through neighboring backyards; she called police, who, next day, working with the woman's description, and other information, arrested Virgil Cantry, thirty-nine, a Sandy Hook resident who lived within a mile of the woman and who'd denied the charges. "I don't believe this," I said numbly. "I know him, he wouldn't do such a thing."

Maxine and the others laughed at me, at the look in my face.

I said, "No! Really. He wouldn't, ever."

I went to hang up my jacket, dazed as if I'd been hit over the head. Behind me I could hear them talking, laughing. That hum and buzz of jubilation.

On my break I ran to police headquarters a few blocks away. I asked to see Virgil Cantry and was told that he wasn't there; he hadn't been arrested, as the *Gazette* had stated, only brought in for questioning. I was excited, upset; I demanded to speak with one of the investigating officers; I told him that Mr. Cantry was a former teacher of mine and we'd been together on Christmas Eve and he couldn't possibly have been the man prowling in backyards. "And Mr. Cantry couldn't run, either. He has a problem with his legs."

I learned that the woman making the complaint had called police at 8:50 P.M. of Christmas Eve. It was ridiculous, I thought, to imagine that Virgil Cantry had gone out after I'd left him, in the condition he was in, to behave in such a desperate way. I insisted we'd been together until 9:30 P.M. I gave an official statement to the Sandy Hook police, signed my name. I was trembling, incensed. I saw that they disliked me, my looks, my excited voice and gestures, but probably they believed me. "It's got to be someone else," I said. "You have no right to harass Mr. Cantry."

Afterward I would learn that Virgil Cantry had been one of several men brought to the station for questioning. Though he hadn't seemed to fit the woman's description of a burly dark-haired man in a leather jacket, with a scruffy beard, police had brought him in anyway since he was one of the few local residents with a police record (for public intoxication, disturbing the peace and resisting arrest nine years before— charges to which he'd pleaded guilty in exchange for probation and fines instead of a prison term). The following week the prowler was sighted again, and arrested.

When Lee Yardboro returned from Boca Raton, trimmer by a few pounds, tanned and ebullient, he was told of the "arrest" of his former customer and how I'd gone to police headquarters, what I'd said. It had become a familiar tale at the diner, repeated frequently, laughed over. Mr. Yardboro thought it was funny, too; he was a man who liked to laugh.

Teasing me, "What, honey, you're Lover Boy's girl? How the hell long's this been going on?"

My face burned as if it was on fire. "No. I just wanted to help him."

"Yeah? But you were with him, you said? Christmas Eve?"

Mr. Yardboro laughed, laughed. His warm heavy hand falling on my shoulder.

In mid-January I discovered a letter for "Xavia," neatly typed, in a plain white envelope slipped into my mail slot.

Dear Xavia,
Thank you. I am deeply grateful to you. But so humiliated. I see I am "fair game" in this terrible place.
Your friend,
Virgil Cantry

I never saw him again, I suppose he moved away from Sandy Hook. But he'd loved me for an hour, at least. I hadn't loved him and that was too bad. But for that hour, I was loved.

One day in late January Mr. Yardboro called me into the kitchen to give me instructions in fish cleaning. One of the kitchen help had just departed the Sandy Hook Diner, there was urgent need for a cook's assistant.

Sucking at a toothpick, Mr. Yardboro pointed to the cleaver already moist with watery blood, and told me to take it up. Eight whole fish had been placed belly up on the butcherblock table. "Start with the heads, sweetheart. Chop-chop! Care-ful. Now the tails. Don't swing crooked. Don't be shy. Good girl!"

My fingers were like ice. I was excited, nervous. Mr. Yardboro smiled at my squeamishness.

Rainbow trout, perch, halibut. These fish were bought unfilleted from the Hoboken supplier because they were much cheaper that way. They were to be gutted and cleaned and deboned and rinsed in cold water and fried in greasy breadcrumbs or baked and stuffed in a gummy substance described in the menu as mushroom-crab dressing which was in fact chopped mushroom stems and that repulsive synthetic food imported from Japan, sealegs.

The fish were slithery-cold. Like snakes. Their scales winked in the bright overhead fluorescent light. Black button-eyes gazing up at me, bland and unblaming. *One day you'll be in this position. You won't feel a thing.*

I swung the heavy cleaver in a wider, wilder arc than Mr. Yardboro wished. The sharp blade neatly decapitated a trout and sank a half-inch into the wood. Mr. Yardboro whistled. "Not so hard, sweetheart. You're a strong girl, eh?"

I laughed, meaning to enjoy this.

The fish-stink was making me slightly nauseated, though. And that ringing in my ears. (I'd been taking diet pills for quick energy.) But I did as Mr. Yardboro instructed, chopping heads and tails and pushing them into a bucket on the floor. Without the round black eyes gazing at me, I performed more capably.

"Now the guts and innards, kid. Go right in."

"Right *in*?"

Mr. Yardboro, who often boasted he'd gone ocean fishing since he'd been a kid, responsible for cleaning his own catch, showed me how it was done. His fingers were stubby but deft and quick. My fingers were stubby but less certain.

I was clumsy. Guts stuck to my fingers. Blood, tissue. Bits of broken bone beneath my nails. I must've reached up to touch my hair. Later I'd discover a strand of translucent fish gut in my hair and I'd figure that was why Mr. Yardboro smiled at me in that way of his.

Next deboning. "Never mind trying to get 100 percent of the bones," Mr. Yardboro said. "This isn't the Ritz." I was clumsier yet, trying to detach fish backbones from raw flesh. And how exquisitely fine these bones. Curving translucent bones, some of them no larger than a hair, a filament. It seemed amazing to me that inside the sleek fish bodies there was a labyrinth of tiny bones. So easily broken by a clumsy human hand. "What're you waiting for? Get rid of that crap."

Quickly I pushed the bones into the bucket. What a stink

arose from that bucket. The kitchen's fans were roaring full blast.

"Okay, honey. Let's see you do the operation by yourself, A to Z. Chop-chop."

Lee Yardboro wasn't much taller than I was but he loomed over me. Slightly crowding me. Nudging my shoulder with his. Like we were equals almost, but I knew better.

Through my life I'd never be able to eat fish without smelling the odors of the Sandy Hook kitchen and feeling a wave of excitement so intense it shaded into nausea. Raw fish guts, fried fish, greasy bread crumbs. I was sickened, but still I ate.

Rachel Wetzsteon

from Home and Away

I

How different any house looks from outside
and from within. I used to circle mansions
finding out, through guessing and good luck,
what acts of kindness kept the home fires warm
and what was done in dens. Now all unpacked
I feel the leaping flame below the floor,
my dreams consist of madly smoking chimneys
turning into smoking guns. All you
who covet life behind closed doors, look out
for changing views: safe homes can be deceiving
and dusty corners, formerly the mark
of depths unsounded, or of time well spent,
become the cold, gray, fuzzy, woolly monsters
that fill the head before an idea forms.

II

I walked among the gorgeous unturned stones
with rising hopes, a pickax and a plan:
the answers I scraped free would be the bricks
I'd use to build a green and spacious home,
and in this place of knowledge I would glue
wild eyes to lush walls, grateful for the gleams
my mystery, my spur had sent my way.
What I could not predict was that there comes
a time when there are no more stones to scrape
the mossy truth from, that a house composed
of all the answers that I schemed so hard
to get could get so gray. My cellmate and

my stone, who could have known that there was such
a thing as knowing someone else too well?

III

Acting in accordance with your wishes,
let us try a quick experiment:
buy a house and set it down on firm soil
and, completing all the steps required,
fill it to the brim with embryo yous.
When little creatures hang from chandeliers
and steal your treasured hours, ask yourself
the reason for the choice: was it to fill
the wanting world with more endangered lives
like yours? Was it to cauterize old wounds?
Was it to see yourself forever blended
with a beloved other? If the first,
sheer hubris; if the second, lots of luck;
if the third, when water blends with oil.

IV

The oldest story in the book has just
revealed another chapter. There are no
competitors with bedroom eyes who send
encoded notes; no juvenile excuses;
no trio of bored, beautiful delinquents
who flutter past on bicycles, intent
on cigarettes and scandal. In their place
there is a pyramid without a base
on either side of which, the rival lives
of rugged climber, deity of parks
and doomed, descending homeowner, are stationed.
Sometimes they meet in a productive summit
but even then, they cannot miss the sight
of skating eros, red-faced at the bottom.

V

Something, love, is singing in the shower
but it is not me; all the spouts are on
but rather than warm water, I suspect
a flood of doubts comes crashing on my brain.
Wise fools have always said that when you woo,
a breathing world surrounds you; what they save
for later revelations on the stairwell
is how you stand there, listening for clues
leading to the arrest of household objects.
Accessories I use to tame my hair
remind me of the hairpin turns we used
to skirt; cigar butts, fuming in an ashtray,
form just a tiny portion of the troops
gathering daily in this screaming house.

VI

Provocateurs and spies have been among us,
sensitive eyes who knew what we were up to
when we exhaled tornadoes; and when they were
dead to the world or elsewhere, there were portents:
great gusts of rain approved our resolutions,
sunshine meant watch and wait. But in this big house
nobody seems to notice; I could drop hints,
swallow a capsule or a morning toad,
or I could claw the walls until the day came
and there would still be no one there to see it,
no way of telling my heart was not in it
except the banner of decisive action,
the calling of the sharp, impatient helper
that rattles in the cupboard, set on escape.

VII

Before I stab, a moment of polemic:
little fish, aspiring to be big ones,

cannot observe a couple without smirking,
avidly drain the color from our lives
until there is no unrest in our room
except the paper flame that they would put there
to fuel their furnace: we become an excuse.
Great unveilers, chroniclers of the war zone,
certainly talk of the eternal struggle
over the reins, but for our sake remember
there is no background as explosive as its
passionate foreground: get it through your head that
we are not cloth dolls with holes and bulges
but flesh in houses, killing with our own hands.

VIII

We may have our problems, rash explainer,
but at least we are not walking automata,
holding hands to keep a toiler busy,
getting mad to help a tirade along.
The forces of production knock on our door;
I scare them away by the timbre of my voice.
Ghosts barge in and reshuffle the blood on the wall
until it resembles a toolbit or a mother,
but the blood keeps pumping out; I stab and stab
because of a cruel word said the other day,
a gray hair found in the soap scum, a desire
to stop a head from cracking, and most of all
because of the face that flashes past your lashes
and is not mine. I stab at that flinty tempter.

IX

By this I knew I'd never leave my room
to look at cities, parks or art again:
the carnage was a comfort, not a care,
the thing that lay beside me on the bed
improved my mood because it matched the red
around the house, the red that ruled the world.

But even killers singing odes to gore
have lucid intervals. I thought of all
the faces that I never saw because
I was so busy welding them to views:
the bright eyes raised in ecstasy, the head
hung low in grief—for them I carry a torch
that lights the corners of my chamber as
I wait for sirens, as I wait for sleep.

X

Sometimes the flames remind me of your good points;
other times, when I become too bold
and start believing that you might come visit
they leap as if to say, Thus I refute you.
Who knows whether the things I do without you—
making shadow puppets on the walls,
giving private screenings of my crimes—
will cure me of the urge to do it over?
I only know that sometimes when the flames
are cool enough to walk through, I will risk
the shame of being found out by my keeper,
and the worse shame of never being noticed,
by standing at the red-rimmed, steamy window
through which, sometimes, a park bench will appear.

Four Poems by Nicholas Christopher

On a Clear Night in February

In the Kyi Valley of Tibet, a snow-white desert
where an orchestra of lamas performs by starlight for the gods,
it is said that when we near death, and may least suspect it,
sorcerers disguised as people in our daily lives—
neighbors, postmen, shopkeepers—
steal a single breath from us, slip it into a bag,
and at the moment we expire deposit it
high in the mountains that hold up the sky.

Sometimes the sorcerers can assume the form
of someone even closer to us, a friend or relative,
or a lover opening her handbag on a street corner.
As you are doing now—while the strains
of an orchestra waft from a car radio—
rummaging for your comb, running it through your hair,
and then snapping the bag shut with a smile.
Taking my breath away.

In the Shadow of the Mountain

at a broken table
ringed by potted flowers
between which the spiders have strung bridges
the women push back their chairs
leaving their cold soup untouched

The doors have been removed from their hinges
and the windows are boarded up

in anticipation of the hurricane
that will strip bare
the foliage along the green river

In the failing light dogs in packs
are roaming the beach
owls are streaming ashes from their wings
flowers heavy as stones
are sinking to the ocean floor

Whole slopes of this mountain will be torn away
the boulders where lizards bask at noon
and the banyan trees clotted with myna birds
and afterwards one of the women will return
to the broken table which has remained standing

among the flowerpots and chairs scattered
on the terrace newly laced with spiderwebs
and dip her broken fingers into the single
untouched bowl of soup feeling for the stone
the color of water she found on the mountain

many years ago and lost many years later
shaped like the mountain itself
whose inverted shadow darkening the valley
is approaching slowly now
like a hurricane

Birds of Paradise in Ice Water

In this room where no one speaks above a whisper,
despite the absence of a sick or dying person
or the presence of anyone engaged
in a difficult or private task, a dozen
of the great flowers on their formidable stems

have been arranged in a glass pitcher before a picture
window looking down the snow-covered street.

I have seem them growing wild by the hundreds
along a riverbank on a Pacific island.
As I dipped my oars silently so as not to frighten
birds from their perches, the flowers loomed suddenly,
the slashed-orange petals with their rainbow streaks
indeed like wings poised to take flight
through the curtain of mist descending the mountains.

The canopy on the building at the end of the street
has frozen in place as the wind left it, curling upward,
like a wave cresting to break in the open sea,
and in the vase what appeared to be clear stones anchoring
the stems are in fact ice cubes to keep the flowers crisp
as the day they were cut from steaming soil under a fiery sky
in which hundreds of birds — brighter than fire — were
   wheeling.

Della

After washing your face and leaving it
in the basin of water from which it stared
up at you as you left the room,

you went out into the world where perfect
strangers coming up dazed from the river
waved to you through the deep sunlight.

This was the day on which you passed
the boy with the bandaged hands who wore
a placard that read EYES EXAMINED — 50¢,

and the grim young women in heels and shorts
pushing the empty stroller around
the parking lot in diminishing circles,

and the man in the cardboard box striding into
traffic swinging a plastic lantern, like Diogenes,
and the blind vendor in the skullcap roasting

almonds in honey by the hotel where the married
couple (each married to someone else) who had become
the morning headlines were found back to back under

icy sheets after sharing a bottle of sleeping pills,
and the breezy clerk with ink-stained fingers
and zip-up boots playing ticktacktoe on the #2

express train beside the pregnant girl
who was dreaming openly with an upturned face
and parted lips, hands clasped on her belly;

this was the day your friend Della disappeared
and no one — not friends, family
(her half-sister who hired a shady detective),

or finally the police — ever found her.
And for years, while waiting for the postcard
or phone call from some other city that never came,

you will pick over the details of all you saw
after setting out to meet Della that morning,
arriving at her apartment to find the door open

and her few possessions undisturbed,
her caged bird singing by the window and the sink
full of clear water in which you glimpsed

your face again, just as you had left it
in the room across town, but changed, even then,
before you knew you would never see Della again.

Two Poems by Charles H. Webb

In Praise of Pliny

He tells of headless people with eyes on their shoulders,
dog-headed people who bark, one-legged people
who hop fast, mouthless people fed by the scent
of roots and flowers, whom a stink can kill.

Twenty hours of every twenty-four, Pliny labored
to stuff into his *Historia Naturalis* "the contents
of the entire world." Servants read to him as he ate.
No time to waste, if he was to know how the elk-like

achlis has no knees, and so can not lie down to sleep.
How it runs backwards dragging its huge lip.
How the *mantichora* has a lion's body, scorpion's tail,
and human face with three rows of fangs.

Of the moon, he writes, "now curved into the horns
of a sickle, now rounded into a circle;
spotted, and then suddenly shining clear,
vast and full-orbed, then suddenly not there."

Earth "belongs to men as the sky belongs to God . . .
lavishing what scents and savors, what juices, what surfaces
to touch, what colors." "Where," he wondered,
"did Nature find room in a flea for every sense?"

He tells how to choose good onions, and make glue;
how elephants write Greek, and hyenas call shepherds' names.
To cure a headache, he asserts, crush snails on the forehead,
coat the nose with vulture brains, wrap the temples

with rope used in a suicide. For toothache, gargle
boiled vinegar-and-frogs. For sneezing and hiccups,

kiss a mule's nose. For hair loss, dandruff, thin eyebrows,
rub with sulfur and bull piss. For any ailment: chicken soup.

When Vesuvius blew, Pliny—naval commander,
confidant of Emperors—sailed to Stabiae to save a friend.
He jotted notes as pumice rattled his friend's roof,
and snored all night. Next morning, pillows shielding heads,

his men struggled to launch their boat into high seas.
When flames and sulfur gas swept down, Pliny collapsed.
As he lay dying on the beach, could he have conceived
of people lacking all belief, devoid of wonder—

two-dimensional people who scoff at everything,
and swear their lives are wretched even as they roar
in horseless chariots across the earth he loved,
and soar in winged phalli through the enormous sky?

Tone of Voice

It pinks the cheeks of speech, or flushes the forehead.
It's a spring breeze in which words play, a scorching sun
that burns them red, slate clouds that cover them in ice.
Mastering tone, the child outgrows his sticks and stones.

"*Okay*," he sneers, twisting the word in Mommie's eye.
Ellipses, dashes, all capitals, underlines—
these are tuna nets through which tone's minnows slide.
"I love you" may arrive spiked like a mace, or snickering.

"State your name" from lawyers' lips can mean "You lie!"
Tone leaks the truth despite our bests efforts to hide.
It's verbal garlic; mistress on a husband's hands.
Consider, dear, when you ask, "Where are my french fries?"

how you may stand in a silk teddy holding grapes,
a suit of mail holding a lance, a hangman's hood holding
a rope. As useless to protest, "I didn't mean that,"
as to tell corpse, "Stand up. You misinterpreted my car."

PREFACE

These letters from Hav, originally contributed to the magazine New Gotham, were written during the months leading up to the events, in the late summer of 1985, which put an end to the character of the city. They thus constitute the only substantial civic portrait ever published, at least in modern times. Countless visitors, of course, left passing descriptions. They marvelled at the Iron Dog and the House of the Chinese Master, they pontificated about New Hav, they caught something of the atmosphere in memoirs, in novels, in poetry

> ...the green-grey shape that seamen swear is Hav,
> Beyond the racing tumble of its foam.

Nobody, however, wrote a proper book about the place. It was almost as though a conspiracy protected the peninsula from too frank or thorough a description.

I count myself lucky in having seen it for the first time late in a travelling life, for it was itself a little compendium of the world's experience, historically, aesthetically, even perhaps spiritually. It reminded me constantly of places elsewhere, but remained to the end absolutely, often paradoxically and occasionally absurdly itself.

A manuscript page from the novel Last Letter from Hav.

Jan Morris

The Art of the Essay II

Jan Morris was born James Humphrey Morris on October 2, 1926, in Somerset, England. As recalled in her memoir,

Conundrum, *"I was three or four when I realized that I had been born into the wrong body, and should really be a girl."* First intimations. But he would live as a man for the next thirty-six years, mentioning his sexual confusion only to his wife, Elizabeth, whom he married at twenty-two in Cairo, where he was working for the local Arab News Agency.

Morris left boarding school at the age of seventeen and served for the next five years in the 9th Queen's Lancers, one of Britain's best cavalry regiments. He then moved to Cairo, but soon returned to Britain, attending Oxford for two years before reentering journalism as a reporter for the Times, which assigned him, because no one else was available, to cover the Hillary and Tensing expedition to Mount Everest. At twenty-six, having never before climbed a mountain, he scaled three-quarters (22,000 feet) of Everest to report the first conquest of the mountain. It was a world scoop, and won him international renown. He went on to a distinguished career as a foreign correspondent, for both the Times and the Guardian.

In 1956, he was awarded a Commonwealth Fellowship, which allowed him to travel through America for a year and resulted in his first book: As I Saw the U.S.A. A similar book was published to great acclaim in 1960, The World of Venice, the product of a year's sabbatical in that city with his family. Morris ended his career as a full-time journalist in 1961, in part because of a newspaper policy that prevented him from expanding his journalistic assignments into books. He went on to publish numerous books, including The Road to Huddersfield: A Journey to Five Continents *(1963)*, The Presence of Spain *(1965) and the* Pax Brittanica *trilogy.*

In 1964, there was another change, personal rather than professional: Morris started taking hormone pills to begin his transformation into a female. The process was completed in 1972, when he traveled to Casablanca for the definitive operation. Her first book as Jan Morris, Conundrum, *chronicles the passing from male to female. But when asked to discuss the sex change further, she demurs, preferring to let that account speak for itself and referring to the whole matter simply as* "the conundrum thing." Since then she has published thirteen books, *including* Travels *(1976),* Manhattan '45 *(1987),* Hong Kong *(1988) and two novels,* Last Letter from Hav *(1985) and* Fisher's Face *(1995).*

Divorce necessarily followed the sex change (it is required by British law), although Morris still lives with his former wife, currently in a house in North Wales called Trefan Morys. Morris describes the house in her book Pleasures of a Tangled Life *(1989): "I love it above all inanimate objects, and above a good many animate ones too. . . . It consists in essence simply of two living rooms, each about forty feet long. Both are full of books, and there is a little suite of functional chambers on two floors at one end, linked by a spiral staircase." They have four children.*

At seventy-one, she looks remarkably youthful, perhaps a result of the hormone pills. And she still travels, this summer to Hong Kong to cover the transfer of power from Britain to China. The interview was begun in 1989 under the auspices of the 92nd Street YMHA, at Hunter College in New York City, and continued through telephone calls and letters.

INTERVIEWER

You resist being called a travel writer.

JAN MORRIS

Yes. At least I resist the idea that travel writing has got to be factual. I believe in its imaginative qualities and its potential as art and literature. I must say that my campaign, which I've been waging for ages now, has borne some fruit because intelligent bookshops nowadays do have a stack called something like travel *literature*. But what word does one use?

INTERVIEWER

Writing about place?

MORRIS

Yes, that's what I do. Although I think of myself more as a belletrist, an old-fashioned word. Essayist would do; people understand that more or less. But the thing is, my subject has been mostly concerned with place. It needn't be. I believe my best books to be far more historical than topographical. But like most writers, I think far too much about myself anyway, and in my heart of hearts don't think I am worth talking about in this way.

INTERVIEWER

Basically, what you are then is an historian.

MORRIS

Well, my best books have been histories. That's all.

INTERVIEWER

So let's start with your *Pax Britannica* trilogy. Did you have Gibbon's *Decline and Fall of the Roman Empire* in mind when you began?

MORRIS

No, not at all. When I began the trilogy I didn't know I was going to write it. I ought to tell you how I got into writing it. I'm old enough to remember the empire when it still was the empire. I was brought up in a world whose map was painted very largely red, and I went out into the world when I was young in a spirit of imperial arrogance. I felt, like most British people my age, that I was born to a birthright of supremacy; out I went to exert that supremacy. But gradually in the course of my later adolescence and youth my views about this changed.

INTERVIEWER

Did they change at a particular moment?

MORRIS

Yes. I was living in what was then Palestine, and I had occasion to call upon the district commissioner of Gaza. He was an Englishman. It was a British mandate in those days, and he was the British official in charge of that part of Palestine. I knocked on his door and out he came. Something about this guy's hat made me think twice about him. It was kind of a bohemian hat. Rather a floppy, slightly rakish or raffish hat; a very, very civilian hat—a sort of fawn color, but because it was bleached by imperial suns and made limp by tropical rainstorms all of the empire was in that hat. He seemed to be rather a nice man. I admired him. He had none of my foolish, cocky arrogance at all. He was a gentleman in the old sense of the word. And through him, and through meeting some of his colleagues, I began to see that my imperial cockiness was nonsense and that the empire, in its last years at least, wasn't a bit arrogant, it wasn't a bit cocky. People like that were simply trying to withdraw from an immense historical process and hand it over honorably to its successors. Because of this, my view of the empire changed.

I went on and wrote a book about an imperial adventure, which was a crossing of southeast Arabia, with the Sultan of Oman, but under the auspices of the Raj, really. One of the reviewers of the book said: why does this author fiddle around along the edges, along the perimeters of this imperial subject? Why not get down to the heart of it? For once a writer did take notice of what a reviewer suggested: because of what he said, I decided I'd write a large, celebratory volume at the center of the imperial story, 1897, which was the time of the queen's Diamond Jubilee and the climax of the whole imperial affair. I wrote that book, and I loved doing it. Then I thought, Well, I'll add one on each side of it and make a triptych. I'll have a volume showing how Queen Victoria came to the throne and the empire splurged into this great moment of climax. Then we'll have the climactic piece. Finally, we'll have an elegiac threnody, letting the thing die down until the end, which I took to be the death of Winston Churchill. Nothing at all to do with Gibbon.

INTERVIEWER

In what's now the Queen Victoria volume you demonstrated something you do frequently. You began with the particular, with Emily Eden, and then spread out over the British Empire. The reader sort of grows up with Queen Victoria. In the preface of the first volume you state that you are "chiefly attracted by the aesthetic of empire." Did this dictate a different approach?

MORRIS

Yes, it did. Because I did not set out to exhibit a moral stance about the empire. I treated it as an immense exhibition. By and large, I accepted the moral views of those who were doing it at the time. Things that would seem wicked to us now didn't always seem wicked to people in the Victorian age. I accepted that. Since this is an escapist point of view, really, I decided that I would not in any way make it an analysis of empire but rather an evocation. The looks and smells and sensations of it. What I later tried to imagine was this: supposing in the last years of the Roman Empire one young centurion, old enough to remember the imperial impulses and the imperial splendor but recognizing that it was passing, sat down and wrote a large book about his sensations at that moment. Wouldn't that be interesting? Said I, "But somebody *could* do it about this still greater empire, the British Empire." Who is that? I asked myself. "Me!"

INTERVIEWER

As empire began its decline, more frightening than the loss of territory, you say, was the possibility that the British might have lost the will to rule. In what ways was empire's decline an expression of British character at the time?

MORRIS

In several ways it was. In the more honorable way, I think it was in the way that I was trying to express my responses to the district commissioner of Gaza. There were a great many very decent men who were devoting their lives to the empire. Perhaps, when they began their careers, they did it in a paternalistic way, which is in itself a form of arrogance; by the time I got into it, very few of them were arrogant. They were only anxious to hand it over honorably and at a reasonable speed. I think they did it very well on the whole. Compared with the record of the French leaving their empire, the British did it in a successful, kindly way. But at the same time, of course, the British had been absolutely shattered by two world wars. The first one left the empire physically larger than ever before. The second one was an obvious death knell for it. The British came out of the Second World War an extremely tired and disillusioned nation, exemplified by the fact that they immediately gave the boot to their great hero, Winston Churchill. All they were interested in then was getting back to their island and trying to make it a more decent place to live. In that respect, the will to empire had most certainly gone. And the sense of enterprise and of adventure and of push and of just a touch of arrogance too — of swagger, at least — that had been essential to the extension of the empire. All that had been kicked out of the British. Perhaps a very good thing too.

INTERVIEWER

There was such a show of panache, such a show of grandeur, such pageantry.

MORRIS

You mean the ending of it or the running of it?

INTERVIEWER

The running of it.

MORRIS

The ending of it too was done with a certain panache, a lot of grand pullings down of flags and trumpet calls and royalty going out to kiss prime ministers lately released from jail.

INTERVIEWER

You begin the trilogy as James Morris. The second volume was written during the ten years of sexual ambiguity when you were taking female hormones but had not yet changed your gender. And the third was written as Jan Morris. To what extent is the character of the trilogy seasoned by this change?

MORRIS

I truly don't think at all, really. I've reread the books myself with this in mind. I don't think there is a great deal of difference. It was a purely intellectual or aesthetic, artistic approach to a fairly remote subject. It wasn't anything, I don't think, that could be affected much by my own personal affairs . . . less than other things I've written.

INTERVIEWER

The very heart of this question is: do you feel your sensibilities at all changed?

MORRIS

That is a different question. The trilogy: I started it and finished it in the same frame of mind. But I suppose it is true that most of my work has been a protracted potter, looking at the world and allowing the world to look at me. And I suppose there can be no doubt that both the world's view of me and my view of the world have changed. Of course they have. The point of the book *Pleasures of a Tangled Life* is to try to present, or even to present to myself what kind of sensibility has resulted from this experience. I'm sick to death of talking about the experience itself, as you can imagine, after twenty years. But I've come to recognize that what I am is the result of the experience itself. The tangle that was there is something that has gone subliminally through all my work. The one book I think isn't affected is the *Pax Britannica* trilogy.

INTERVIEWER

At the end of the trilogy you say that you've come to view empire less in historical than in redemptory terms. What do you mean?

MORRIS

I was thinking of Teilhard de Chardin's concept of "infurling," in which he thought that history, by a process of turning in upon itself, was very gradually bringing humanity and nature into a unity. When I was in Canada I came across an old newspaper article about a lecture on imperialism given in about 1902. Nearly all imperialist talk of that time was about the majesty of the British economic power or the strength of the navy. But this one wasn't at all; this lecturer viewed empire as an agent of love. He thought that among all these mixed emotions there was a common thread of love — of people being fond of each other and trying to do the best for each other. And I've come to think that the good is simply more resilient than the bad. If you have a great historical process like the British Empire, the bad is dross; it is thrown away. The good is what stays on. There was some good in imperialism. It did enable people to get to know each other better than they had before. It allowed people to break away from shackling old traditions and heritages. It introduced the world to fresh ideas and new opportunities. These are the contributions that matter for the redemption and the unity of us all. Although I am at heart against empires, I do think that the British did leave behind them a great number of friends.

INTERVIEWER

At the end of the trilogy you ask, "Is that the truth? Is that how it was? It is my truth. Its emotions are mine. Its scenes are heightened or diminished by my vision. If it is not invariably true in the fact, it is certainly true in the imagination." In what way is this statement true of any history?

MORRIS

Oh, I think it can be untrue of some histories . . . There are people who write history as a deliberate distortion because they want to deliver a message or shove over a creed. Mine wasn't false in that sense. I tried to present both sides of the story. I didn't try to distort anything to fit another purpose.

INTERVIEWER

I was thinking of that extra inch or half-inch that Lytton Strachey added onto the archbishop. Such is the temptation when one is writing history: to add that extra inch.

MORRIS

Of course, there is one small distortion in my kind of history in that it aims to entertain. So it does in effect ignore little matters like economics. But I have a story too. In *Pleasures*, I have a piece about first enjoying food and drink. Until I was in my mid-twenties, I didn't take much interest in them. But when I lunched in Australia at the famous cartoonist George Molnar's house on the lawn overlooking Sydney Harbor, the meal was something quite simple but delicious: pâté, crusty rolls, a bottle of wine, an apple, this sort of thing. There was something about the way this man presented and served the food. He crunched the bread in sort of a lascivious way. He spread the pâté kind of unguently. He almost slurped the wine. I thought it was so marvelous. When I came to describe it, I could see it all again so clearly: the dancing sea, the clear Australian sky, the green lawn; above us were the wings of the Sydney opera house, like a benediction over this experience. It was only when I finished the chapter that I remembered that the Sydney opera house hadn't been built yet!

INTERVIEWER

I would like to ask you about *The World of Venice*. Judging from the book and from the entire trilogy, you seem supremely interested in declines and falls. Are you trying to tell us about the decline and fall of the whole world, of reality in our time? And if so, is there any new beginning?

MORRIS

I certainly don't think that I'm trying to describe the decline and fall of the world. Rather, it seems more vigorous as every year goes by. Perhaps, it is because I am aware of the excitement of the present age—the explosive beauty of the new technologies that are overcoming us, the vivacity of the world—that I am attracted to decline, to the melancholy spectacle of things that get old and die. But another reason I tend to write about decline is because I don't believe in pretending it doesn't exist. I believe in age; I believe in recognizing age. I'm sure that I shall always love Venice, but in a way I do wish it wasn't being touched up. I think it's trying to deny its age, pretending that it isn't antiquated and decrepit, which it is, really. One part of me is very attracted to that decline, and another part of me is fascinated by the fact that Venice denies that decline so adamantly. Such a scenario is not part of my view of the world in the 1990s. Rather, I take the opposite stance. I see the world today as in a very vigorous, virile and interesting state.

INTERVIEWER

You first published *The World of Venice* in 1960 as James Morris. In the preface to the 1974 reprinted edition, you, as Jan Morris, see the book as a period piece: "Venice seen through a particular pair of eyes at a particular moment," which "cannot be modernized with a few deft strokes of a felt-tip pen." Would Jan have written a different book than James?

MORRIS

It's extremely hard to say. As a reprint it was no longer a contemporary portrait of the city because a lot had changed in the meantime. I resigned myself to the fact that the Venice I had described was my Venice, really. As to whether Jan Morris would write the book differently . . . I used to think that as Jan I tend to concentrate more on the smaller things, the details, rather than on the grand sweep of things. But as I've got older, I've come to think that the grand sweep and the details are exactly the same; the macrocosm and the microcosm are identical.

INTERVIEWER

You speak of the book on Venice as "a highly subjective, romantic, impressionistic picture, less of a city than of an experience." Is that true of any city you portray? Is it more true in some cases than in others?

MORRIS

It's true of them all, certainly. I'm not the sort of writer who tries to tell other people what they are going to get out of the city. I don't consider my books travel books. I don't like travel books, as I said before. I don't believe in them as a genre of literature. Every city I describe is really only a description of me looking at the city or responding to it. Of course, some cities have a more brilliant image. In this case the city overtakes me so that I find I am not, after all, describing what I feel about the city but describing something very, very powerful about the city itself. For example, Beijing: I went to that city in my usual frame of mind, in which I follow two precepts. The first I draw from E.M. Forster's advice that in order to see the city of Alexandria best one ought to wander around aimlessly. The other I take from the psalms; you might remember the line: "Grin like a dog and run about the city."

INTERVIEWER

And scare the hell out of the populace!

MORRIS

Yes. Well, I went into Beijing wandering aimlessly and grinning like a dog and running about in the usual way, but it didn't work! Beijing was too big for me. Its size imposed upon what I wrote about the city.

INTERVIEWER

In the introduction to your collection of writings about cities you say that you've accomplished at last what you set out to do.

MORRIS

I drew an imaginary, figurative line between two cities, Budapest and Bucharest. All cities above that line qualify as what seem to me "great cities," and all below that line could be very interesting but not in the same class. So I resolved that before I died I would visit and write about all the cities above the Bucharest line. I could do some below if I wanted to, but I would try to do all the ones above. In the end I did. Beijing was the last one.

INTERVIEWER

Is there any place you haven't written about that you would like to?

MORRIS

I think I'm tired of writing about places qua places—if I ever did that. But I've never been into Tibet proper (only on the frontier) and I would like to go there; also Vladivostok: both places where the situation would be as interesting to write about as the locality.

INTERVIEWER

Is there any place you have been unable to capture?

MORRIS

I always think London has defeated me: probably heaps of other places too—who am I to judge?

INTERVIEWER

You say that by 1980 you had fallen out of love with Venice. What happened?

MORRIS

I fall in and out of love with Venice very frequently as a matter of fact. I've known Venice since the end of the Second World War. For most of that time Venice has been trying to find a role for itself, to be a creative, living city or to be a kind of museum city that we all go and look at. At one time it was intended to be a dormitory town for the big industrial complex around the lagoon and Mestre. That fell through because of pollution, so Venice was out on a limb again. The attempt to bring it into the modern world had failed. Then one day I saw that the golden horses of Saint Mark's were no longer on the facade of the basilica. They'd taken the statues down and put them inside. Outside they'd placed some dummies . . . good replicas but without the sheen and the scratches, the age and the magic of the old ones. I thought, This is the moment when Venice has decided. It won't be a great diplomatic, mercantile or political city, nor will it be a great seaport of the East. Instead it will be a museum that we can all visit. Maybe that's the right thing for it, anyway. Age has crept up on it. It can't do it anymore. Perhaps that's the answer. For a time I went along with that, but in the last five or ten years mass tourism has taken such a turn, especially in Europe and particularly in Venice. It seems to me that the poor old place is too swamped with tourism to survive as even a viable museum unless it takes really drastic steps to keep people out.

INTERVIEWER

Still, there are strange haunted squares in Venice that one can find, away from tourists.

MORRIS

There are haunted squares where one can sit in Indianapolis!

INTERVIEWER

Those dummy horses are very significant to me too, but to me they meant something slightly different. They seemed to be symbols of the decline and fall of reality in my time.

MORRIS

If it is true about the decline and fall of reality, then its chief agency is tourism. Tourism encourages unreality. It's easier in the tourist context to be unreal than real. It's the easiest thing in the world to buy a funny old Welsh hat and pop it on and sit outside selling rock in some bogus tavern. It's much easier than being real, contemporary. Tourism encourages and abets this shamness wherever it touches. I detest it.

INTERVIEWER
For those who don't know what *rock* is, it's a very sweet candy.

MORRIS
And it can have the name of the place written all the way through it. However much you chew it, it still says Wales. Wales, Wales, Wales.

INTERVIEWER
In your book *Conundrum* you answer almost every conceivable question about your decision to change your gender and the process involved. Your life seems made up of journeys, both in terms of travel and of personal exploration. To what extent was travel a relief or escape from feeling trapped in a man's body?

MORRIS
You mean just ordinary travel, don't you, not travel in a metaphysical sense?

INTERVIEWER
We can come to metaphysical travel later.

MORRIS
Well, I used to think it hadn't anything to do with escape because I've always enjoyed traveling; it's one of my great pleasures. My original travels were not quite voluntary. I went abroad with the British army, and there wasn't much sense of escape in that. But later I did begin to believe that maybe there was some sort of allegorical meaning to my traveling. I thought that the restlessness I was possessed by was, perhaps, some yearning, not so much for the sake of escape as for the sake of quest: a quest for unity, a search for wholeness. I certainly didn't think of it that way in the beginning, but I've come to think it might be so.

INTERVIEWER

From what I know of you, both personally and through your writing, I think it must be so.

MORRIS

I've become obsessed with the idea of reconciliation, particularly reconciliation with nature but with people too, of course. I think that travel has been a kind of search for that, a pursuit for unity and even an attempt to contribute to a sense of unity.

INTERVIEWER

Your description of climbing Mount Everest is such an extraordinary symbolic venture.

MORRIS

Well, it's nice to have it thought as symbolism, but I really don't think of it that way. It was just an assignment, and I did it.

INTERVIEWER

So you have nothing to say about metaphysical travel then?

MORRIS

No, because it seems to me such an inner, indeed inmost matter that, old pro as I am, I can't put it into words.

INTERVIEWER

Is there a book you've written as Jan that James would not have written?

MORRIS

Pleasures of a Tangled Life. The whole point of this book of essays is to try to present the sensibility that has been created or has evolved out of "the conundrum experience," as we say in our evasive, euphemistic way. People who come to interview me at home often ask, "Do you mind if we talk about the conundrum thing?" The book tries to present, to readers as well as myself, what kind of a sensibility has resulted from this sort of thing. I think the conundrum aspect runs subliminally through the whole book. I recognize that the pleasures, nearly all of them, are ones that I enjoy in a particular way because of "the conundrum thing."

INTERVIEWER

Let's talk about *Sydney*. How do you prepare yourself for a particular book?

MORRIS

First of all I decide why I want to write the book. The reason I wanted to write *Sydney* gets me back to the good old empire once again. It seems to me that when the tide of empire withdrew it left behind on the sands of the world a whole lot of objects, some of them unpleasant, some of them dull, but one of them particularly glittering. Not the nicest object, rather a sharp, hard object, but a brilliant one. And that seemed to me the city of Sydney, New South Wales, a city which is not only a remnant of that old empire but also, in a way, the New City. It is creating new people in the same way that America created new people in the 1780s. So I decided that would be a good book to do. I wanted to conclude my commitment, my obsession with the empire. And I thought Sydney was a good place to end with. Somebody reviewing *Sydney* said that most of the books I'd written were cousins to empire in some way; they're related.

INTERVIEWER

At what point during the progress of the book do you feel that you've captured your subject, that the place is yours?

MORRIS

It varies. I usually write the first draft in a sort of stream-of-consciousness way, without thinking very hard about it. I let it all go through. Then when I go back to the second draft, very often I find that what I've already got is much better than what I've planned. Sometimes the unconscious bit is very much better than the conscious bit. I'm a weak person, and so I do, in fact, always replace the unconscious with the conscious bit, but I'm often wrong in doing so. Sometimes I go back and see that the early draft is better and more natural. Incidentally, talking of stream of consciousness, after forty years of trying I've finished Joyce's *Ulysses*. I must say I still think life is too short for *Finnegans Wake*.

INTERVIEWER

Do you feel you got to the *bottom* of Sydney in this book?

MORRIS

No, I don't think so. I got to the bottom, as I say, of my own feelings about it. Sydney is not a city that at first sight is going to incite one's sensibilities. It wants to be frank, macho, fun, you know. But the more I felt the city, the more I thought about the city, the more I realized that sort of *wistful* quality in it, which perhaps is behind all such macho places, really.

INTERVIEWER

A wistful quality?

MORRIS

Yes. It's a kind of yearning. Often what I feel about the Australians themselves is that they resist it a bit because they don't feel they ought to feel these sort of feelings. But they probably do, really, I think. It has something to do with the landscape. D.H. Lawrence got it all those years ago.

INTERVIEWER

But when you have a city, such as Sydney, that's a little bit elusive in terms of its wistful quality, how does that reveal itself to you? Is the realization an active process on your part, or is it something that just flowers as you spend time there?

MORRIS

I think that it is purely passive. All I do, really, is to go to the place and just think about nothing else whatever except that place. I have to say in the case of Sydney that if its transcendental quality hadn't emerged the book might have been a little bit boring. I didn't know it was going to show itself. I felt it more and more the longer I stayed there.

INTERVIEWER

So it wasn't an immediate transcendence?

MORRIS

No. A lot of people see *Sydney* as if it were a "road to Damascus" experience. It wasn't.

INTERVIEWER

You use anecdotes and stories in certain places to punctuate the narrative. Do you consciously use the techniques of fiction to move a narrative along?

MORRIS

I do believe in the techniques of fiction, so I'm very gratified you should ask this. I really don't see that there's much difference between writing a book of this kind and writing a novel. The situations that arise are the sort of situations you'd often make up—the background you would devise for a novel, the characters you would produce for a novel. And you have an added attraction, of course: the fact that the overwhelming character of the whole book is the city itself, which is an advantage you have over the novelist. Paul Theroux said to me once that he liked writing travel books because they gave him a plot; he didn't have to think one up. It works the other way around too. I edited the travel writings of Virginia Woolf. *To the Lighthouse* is in many ways a travel book: the descriptions of the journey across the bay, the views that she provides, are exactly what she would do if she were writing a work of literary travel.

INTERVIEWER

What aspect did the sensibility and change of sensibility based on "the conundrum experience," which you discussed in *Pleasures of a Tangled Life*, play in writing *Sydney*?

MORRIS

Well, of course, *Pleasures of a Tangled Life* was a very much more varied book. It dealt specifically with personal aspects of life, personal views: what happened to me at home, how I feel about different aspects of life and of living and of art and of religion . . . So, naturally, that presents a sensibility far more directly, doesn't it, more immediately, than a book like *Sydney*. On the other hand, I think if you compare with a compassionate eye, a sympathetic eye, a book like *Sydney* with a book like *Oxford*, which I wrote in 1965, I think you would think, if you were intelligent enough, that there was a different person writing. You might not think the style had changed enormously, but I think you'd find the mind behind it or the feeling behind it, the sensibility behind it, had changed. Yes, I think I would think that about *Sydney*. It's a gentler book, of course.

INTERVIEWER

When you're researching a book, do you travel alone?

MORRIS

I generally travel alone, but sometimes with my partner, with whom I've lived for forty years. But dearly though I love her, if I'm going to be working I find I'm better on my own. Love is rather inhibiting in my view. We are always thinking about what each other wants to do. Whereas, to be writing about a place you've got to be utterly selfish. You've only got to think about the place that you're writing. Your antenna must be out all the time picking up vibrations and details. If you've got somebody with you, especially somebody you're fond of, it doesn't work so well. So, although I never have the heart to tell her this, I would really rather not have her come along.

INTERVIEWER

If you're going to be any kind of writer you've got to be utterly selfish.

MORRIS

And lonely, I suppose.

INTERVIEWER

How long do you stay in a place?

MORRIS

That depends entirely on the nature of the thing that I'm writing. If I'm commissioned by a magazine to write an essay, what I do is go to the place for a week and think about nothing but that place. And then, the last few days, in a kind of frenzy of ecstasy or despair, I write three drafts of the essay, one draft each day. I write continuously — it doesn't matter how many hours — until the thing is done. I love the feeling of wrapping the whole thing up, popping it off in the post and going somewhere else. It is very satisfying. I do think that the impact of it, the suddenness and abruptness of it, makes it go better.

The best book about a place I've ever written is the one about Spain. I hardly knew Spain, but I was commissioned to go there for six months to write a book about it. So I bought a Volkswagen camper-bus, and off I set to this country that I knew nothing about. The impact was tremendous; I thought about nothing but Spain for the entire six months. When it was finished I remember watching an airplane going overhead and thinking, There goes my lovely manuscript, on its way to New York. That book, because it was done in a mood of high ecstasy and excitement, was the best of the lot.

INTERVIEWER

How does your mood affect your impression of a place? What you write about it?

MORRIS

I am nothing if not a professional, and I long ago learned to aim off for mood, weather or chance encounters: but of course if I spent a week somewhere with a permanent headache, in perpetual drizzle, encountering only grumpy citizens, I can see that my essay might not be as exuberant as it might be.

INTERVIEWER

You mentioned being lonely . . .

MORRIS

Yes. Well, I'm not lonely when I travel, but, like every writer, I'm a bit lonely when I have to sit down and write the thing, because you can only do that by yourself. I do it rather laboriously, three times over. It's a long process. During that time I'm pretty reclusive and shuttered. But traveling, no, less so than it used to be, really, because, you know, I've been doing it an awfully long time. Wherever I go now I know people. So there's no need for me to be lonely if I don't want to be lonely. The lonely part of it is the technicality of being a writer, which is naturally a lonely one anyway. You can't talk to people while you're writing. You can't work while the television is on.

INTERVIEWER

You could have music.

MORRIS

Lately I bought a little electronic keyboard so that every now and then I break off and play something.

INTERVIEWER

What do you play?

MORRIS

Sometimes if I've got the score, I play the solo part of concertos. I'm very good on the Mendelssohn violin concertos.

INTERVIEWER

How important are languages? How many languages do you speak and to what extent is that critical in investigating a place?

MORRIS

Well, it has been crucial in a way in my choice of subjects. Because so much of my time has been spent with the British Empire and its cousinships, English was the lingua franca so that was no problem. But because I am a poor linguist I've done very few — no books, really, except *Venice* — about cities where the foreign language is essential. I speak sort of pidgin French and Italian. I learned some Arabic years ago, but that wouldn't, for example, qualify me to write a book about Moscow or Berlin, would it? And unlike some of my colleagues, I'm not sure I've got the dedication to learn an entirely new language in order to write a book about that country. Colin Thubron, for example, to write a book about traveling through China actually sat down and learned Mandarin.

INTERVIEWER

So what did you do, say, when you were investigating Venice? Did you use translators?

MORRIS

Well, I'm not too bad on Italian. Do you know that story: Hemingway said what an easy language Italian was, and his Italian friend said, "In that case, Mr. Hemingway, why not undertake the use of grammar?"! When I went to Spain, commissioned to do a short, sixty-thousand-word book, I bought a recorded language course. And the book's been in print ever since.

INTERVIEWER

Has technology, notably the advent of the word processor, changed your technique or style in any way?

MORRIS

I do use a word processor, but it hasn't changed my writing in any way whatever. The belief that style and mental capacity depend upon the instrument one uses is a superstition. I will write with anything at any time. I've used them all — the fountain pen, manual typewriter, electric typewriter — and none have made the slightest difference. But with a word processor I won't type the first few drafts on disk because there is the temptation simply to fiddle with the text, to juggle with it. The word processor is useful to me only for the final draft of the thing. I do think that the word processor for a writer's last draft is a wonderful thing because you can go on and on polishing the thing.

INTERVIEWER

Do you feel that having been a man at one time in your life gives you more courage to make excursions on your own?

MORRIS

Yes. There's a hangover from the confidence I had as a man. When I started, the feminist movement hadn't really happened, so, of course, there was more of a gulf between a male and female traveler. Now things are very, very different. Many women are unnecessarily timid about travel. I don't believe it is so different for a woman or a man nowadays. Of course, there are actual physical dangers of a different kind. But the general run of hazard is exactly the same for men as for women, and the treatment that a woman gets when traveling is, by and large, better. People are less frightened of you. They tend to trust you more. The relationship between women, between one woman and another, is a much closer one than the relationship between men. Wherever a woman travels in the world she's got a few million friends waiting to help her.

INTERVIEWER

You say that you read about and study a place you've never been to before going there to write about it. Do you find that the place turns out to be largely what you expect it to be or exactly what you did not expect it to be?

MORRIS

It's a long time since I've had to write about a place I didn't know. Nowadays, I generally write about places I know about already. But I think some of the great travel books have not prepared me for the place I'm going to. One of them is one of my favorite books, Doughty's *Arabia Deserta*: it's a marvelous book and a great work of art, but the image it presents of the desert and its life isn't the image I felt. I'm not grumbling at all. He wasn't trying to tell me what *I* was going to see in the desert. He was just telling me what the desert was like to him. But that's one book that doesn't seem to match up to my own conceptions of the desert. Sterne, for example, too. I can't say that France seems very much like *A Sentimental Journey* to me. There are some other people too, like Kingslake, who wrote deliberately in an entertaining mode, consciously painting an arresting picture of life. It isn't much like it when you get there.

INTERVIEWER

Back to the dissolution of empires. We've watched the waning and extinction of another great empire, the Soviet Union.

MORRIS

The tragedy of the Soviet Union was that it marked the decline of an ideological empire. The British Empire really had no ideology, except one that had evolved by a kind of rule of thumb, changing as it went along. There was a general rule of fair play about it. But the moral purpose behind the Soviet Empire seems to have been a different thing altogether. I've always been very attracted to the idea of Communism. If I'd been alive in those days I probably would have been a Communist. The tragedy of it was, it seems to me, that it was so soon perverted. The revolution was betrayed. It sank into the horrors of Stalinism, sliding slowly into the awful mires of inefficiency, disillusion, unhappiness and despair that we see now. The failure of it seems to be that although it set out ideologically to provide welfare for a people, it utterly lacked the idea of giving its people happiness. If political ideology doesn't take into account the human desire for happiness, it seems to me bound to fail. Perhaps this is why your system is so successful, because it actually does talk about the pursuit of happiness, doesn't it? That's a different matter altogether.

INTERVIEWER

I once met someone who had visited London and had refused to go back so as not to obliterate the memory she had of it twenty-eight years earlier. Have you ever felt that way about any place?

MORRIS

Yes, I think I have. I've often had doubts about going back, but I find that often they are ill-founded. Chicago is one of them. I first went to Chicago in 1953, and I've been commissioned several times since then to go back. Each time I thought, This is a mistake. It's not going to be what you thought it was; you'll be disappointed. But it wasn't so. Recently I wrote a very long essay about it, and it came off just as well as it had in previous times. Although in principle I agree with your friend, in practice it doesn't seem to be true.

INTERVIEWER

Why do you think Chicago works so well for you? Has it changed?

MORRIS

Yes, of course, it has changed enormously since I first went there, but it's not the change that excites me; it's the sameness—the fact that it still feels like most of us foreigners really want America to feel. There's a touch of an immensely urbane, sophisticated Norman Rockwell to Chicago that we innocents like.

INTERVIEWER

You've called Chicago the perfect city. Is that still true?

MORRIS

I don't think I said perfect. What I do mean is that, among twentieth-century cities, Chicago comes nearest to the ideal of a perfect city . . . an aesthetically perfect city. The shape of it seems to me fine and logical, and the buildings are magnificent. It is the most underrated of all the metropolises of the world in my opinion. I don't think many people say, "I must go and look at that Chicago!" Dickens did, though. As he drove in by train the conductor came through and said, "Mr. Dickens, you're entering the boss city of the universe."

INTERVIEWER

You've written thirty-two books to date, by our count eighteen as James, fourteen as Jan. You've accomplished everything you set out to do?

MORRIS

By no means. There's one particular thing I've failed to do. This experience of mine which every now and then crops up . . . I think I've failed to use it artistically in the way I might have used it. A sex change is a very extraordinary thing for someone to have gone through and particularly extraordinary for a writer, I think. But although, as I say and you recognize, the effects of it appear kind of subliminally through everything I've written, I don't believe I've created a work of art around it.

I think *Fisher's Face* was, as some percipient critics saw, a kind of artistic product of this predicament—it is my favorite among my books—but I still haven't devised any more explicit way of using it. Perhaps I've left it too late?

—Leo Lerman

Aliens of Affection

Padgett Powell

All along the watchtower—which he had never been on before and now that he was on it could not imagine what it was, or what it looked like, or what he looked like on the watchtower, other than the way he usually looked—Mr. Albemarle patrolled. At each end of his walk, or watch, or beat— he had no idea what you called the path he trod until the fog suggested he turn back and trod until the fog at the other end suggested he turn back again—Mr. Albemarle crisply about-faced, having seen and heard nothing. He was on the top of a wall, as near as he could tell, which was one of several walls, as near as he could tell, constituting a garrison, or fort, or prison, or, as near as he could tell, someone's corporate headquarters. Where or how the term *watchtower* had obtained and why, he did not know. He was not on a tower, and if he watched anything it was that he not step off the wall into the cool gauzy air and fall he had no idea how far down onto he had no idea what. If he was on a watchtower, he could only surmise there was a moat, ideally with something dangerous in it, below. But he had no actual vision of anything, and no idea why he was on the watchtower, or whatever it was, no idea why he was walking it and no idea what he was watching for. He had an idea only about why the phrase *all along the watchtower* kept playing in his head: he'd heard it on the radio.

What he seemed to be doing, more than watching or towering or guarding, was modeling. He kept seeing himself stroll and turn in the fog on the wall as if he were on a runway, and he had multiple angled views of himself as if he were turning around before the tripartite mirror in a clothing store. There he was: some kind of guard (for what?) showing, mostly to himself, some clothes that looked strange on him, or not, that he would buy, or not, and have put in a bag, or not; he might wear them out of the store with his old clothes in a bag. That moment had given him a good feeling as a young man — wearing, as it were, virgin clothes fresh from the rack to the street, his old sodden worn duds in a lowly sack at his side. There were no pleasures, large or small, in his life now. He had mismanaged his affections.

All along the watchtower, then, in the fog, he watched, he supposed, for affection. That was the enemy. It was in the belly of a beautiful gift, companionship, which gift was always good to receive until this monster of happiness began to pour out of it and run amok and make him so happy that he betrayed it. Nothing so sweet as true affection could be trusted. True affection is too good to be true. It contains, perforce, disaffection. He walked his wall, all along the watchtower. The fog was lustrous and rising and a comfort. Mr. Albemarle pronounced, orated really, as though he were Hamlet, or some other rarefied speaker, which he was not, the following speech into the fog, aware that loud disputations of this sort surely violated the prescribed duties, whatever they were, of those who perambulate the watchtower: "My specialty is the mismanagement of affections. A cowboy of the heart, I head 'em up and move 'em out: lowing, bellowing, grunting, snorting emotions of slow stupid tenderness driven in mad droves to their end. All you need for this, in the way of equipment, is a good strong horse between your legs. I am a cowboy, or as they say in Sweden, a cawboy. Caw."

Some sodiers showed up. "Hey! Cawboy!" they said, or one of them said. It was a sudden foggy profusion of boots and nylon webbing and weapon noise, all halt-who-goes-there, etc. Mr. Albemarle defended himself against soldiers by calling them, in his mind, sodiers. He defended himself against not ever having been one and the possible indictment of manhood that might constitute, and he defended himself against their potential menace now—as they halted him when he should have been halting them by the terms of his not clearly understood position all along the watchtower—by calling them, in his mind, sodiers. The sodiers said, "Hey, cawboy, you got any cigarettes?"

Mr. Albemarle did and shared them all around and they were immediate fast friends, he and the sodiers.

"You sodiers are okay fine," he boldly said to them.

"We know it," they said, lifting their heavy steel helmets to reveal beautiful multicolored denim welder's caps on backwards on each of their heads. They all smiled, each revealing one missing central incisor, right or left. There were nine sodiers and Mr. Albemarle did not have time to get a count, how many right, how many left incisors missing. He had once considered dentistry as a sop to his mother's hopes for him. A dentist talked him out of it. "I clean *black gunk* out of people's mouths all day, son." That did it. The same dentist, it occurred to him now, had earlier talked him out of being a sodier. "All you do is say,'You three guys go behind that truck and shoot the enemy.' What's there to learn in that?"

This was a sufficiently strong argument, with the black gunk looming as well, to talk young Mr. Albemarle out of enlisting in ROTC and getting educational benefits to allow him to go to dental school. The final straw was the dentist's asking him what he, the dentist, might do about his sagging breasts. His years of cleaning black gunk, slumped over patients on a short stool on wheels, had not maintained a firm tone in the dentist's pectoral muscles, and they indeed drooped, reminiscent of a budding girl's breasts. Mr. Albemarle, who was then eighteen and in fine shape himself and not called yet Mr. Albemarle, told the dentist to lift weights, but to his knowledge the dentist never took his advice.

"You sodiers have good shit, it looks," Mr. Albemarle said.

"We have very good shit," they said. They each searched themselves and gave to Mr. Albemarle a piece of gear. He received from them, all of them standing all along the watchtower and blowing exhales of white smoke into the white fog, a collapsing titanium mess cup with Teflon coating on it that was very sexy to the touch, a boot knife that was too sharp to put in your boot, an OD green tube of sun block, a jungle hammock, with roof and mosquito netting, a pair of very fine, heavy socks (clean), a box of 9 mm shells, an athletic supporter, a flak vest, and a jammed M16 rifle that the sodiers thought was easily fixable but for the life of all of them they could not fathom how.

Mr. Albemarle put on and strapped on all of his new gear and passed around more cigarettes in a truly warm spirit. "Do you sodiers," he asked, "know anything about all-along-the-watchtowering?"

"What do you mean?" they asked.

"Like, what I'm supposed to do."

The sodiers looked at Mr. Albemarle and briefly at each other. "You *doing* it, dude," one of them said, and the others agreed.

"All right, I can accept that," Mr. Albemarle said. "But there is a certain want of certainty regarding just *what* it is I'm doing."

"Well put," a sodier said.

"We are in a not dissimilar position ourselves," said another, to general nodding all along the watchtower.

"We worry it not," a third said.

"A constituent of the orders—"

"To not know—"

"Precisely what we are about."

"So we just, as men with balls and ordnance must, go about the business at hand, whatever it is."

"And we suggest you do too."

This made fine sense to Mr. Albemarle. "One more question

of you fine fellows, then," he said. "Down there—" he pointed down and over the edge of the wall—"any idea what's down there?"

"Moat," a sodier said, "with something dangerous in it."

"That's what I thought," Mr. Albemarle said. "Any idea what?"

"Crocodiles."

"I think badly deteriorated scrap metal, like thousands of bicycles, cut you to ribbons."

"Get tetanus before you hit the water."

"Definitely."

"Get a booster, dude, you plan on swimming in that moat."

"I don't *plan* on swimming in that moat," Mr. Albemarle said. At this the sodiers laughed solidly and loudly, approving of Mr. Albemarle's prudence.

They all shook hands, and Mr. Albemarle thanked them for the gifts, and they him for the smokes, and the sodiers decamped. Mr. Albemarle was feeling good. It had been a fine rendezvous all along the watchtower, and as he resumed his pointless patrol, he patted and slapped all of his fine new gear, more ready now than ever before for whatever it was he was ready for.

"I prefer the cloudy day to the sunny day," he announced toward the moat, trying to detect from any echo if it were crocodiles or bicycles down there, or anything at all. No sound came back.

Some aliens showed up. This was clear, immediately, to Mr. Albemarle. That they were aliens made sudden eminent sense of his theretofore murky task. He had been all along the watchtower watching for aliens. No one could have specified this without appearing to be crazy. Mr. Albemarle understood everything, or nearly everything, now.

The aliens were very forthcoming. They looked perfectly alien, no bones about it. All gooshy and weird, etc. They made calming hand gestures, inducing Mr. Albemarle not to raise his jammed M16 in their direction. They slid up to him as if on dollies and said, "We are aliens. We are aliens of affection."

"What?"

"We are the secret agents, as it were, in cases of alienation of affection."

Mr. Albemarle said, "You mean, when a man finds his wife naked on another man's sailboat and he sues the yachtsman for alienation of affection—"

"Yes. We are in attendance."

"We are on that boat, usually," said another alien of affection.

The first alien slapped this second alien upside the head with a flipper-like arm. "We are *always* on that boat."

Mr. Albemarle offered the aliens of affection cigarettes and looked at them closely. In terms of gear, they were without. In terms of clothes, they were without, yet you would not, Mr. Albemarle considered, be inclined to regard them as naked. The slapped alien appeared ready to accept a cigarette until he received a stern look from the first alien and put his arms, or flippers, approximately where his pants pockets would have been had he had on any pants. Mr. Albemarle reflected upon—actually the thought was exceedingly brief, but trenchant—the apparent absence of genitalia on these aliens of affection. To his mind, affection and genitalia were closely bound up. The notion of secret agents of affection without genitals struck him as either ironic in the extreme or extremely fitting. He looked closely at the slapped alien, up and down, to see if there were misplaced genitals, if that would be the correct term. He saw none.

"What do aliens of affection do?" he asked, aware only after he did so that he might be forward in his asking.

"We alienate affection," the first alien said.

"There's Cupid and there's us," the second said. Mr. Albemarle expected him to receive another slap for this remark, which struck him as impertinent, or low in tone, but there was no objection shown by any of the other aliens. There were nine of them, as there had been nine sodiers. Mr. Albemarle was unable to detect the status of missing incisors because he could not determine, watching them speak, if they had teeth at all, or, really, mouths. They were weird, as he supposed was fitting. They were so weird that they weren't weird, because aliens are supposed to be weird, and they *were* weird so they *weren't* weird. He liked them, rather, but he was not as fond of them as he had been of the sodiers. They did not give him any gear, but beyond that they did not give him any comfort. Why should they? he thought. He had mismanaged his affections, and now it appeared feasible these guys might have had something to do with it. Every time he had broken a heart, or had his broken, maybe one of these gremlins had been there aiding and abetting, helping him fuck up. Perhaps this was the enemy. Perhaps these thalidomide-looking wizened things were why he was walking all along the watchtower in an ill-defined mission, preferring cloudy days to sunny.

"Let's take a reading on Loverboy here," the first alien said, and very quickly the slapped alien was very close to Mr. Albemarle. He had in the popular expression invaded Mr. Albemarle's air space, as had once a homosexual photographer who stood inches from him with wet lips and gleaming eyes and asked, "Do I make you nervous?" Nervous, Mr. Albemarle of course said, "No." Another time his air space had been invaded by a turkey in a barnyard, a big cock turkey or whatever you called the male, which could in raising its feathers expand itself about 300 percent and make you pee in your pants if you were, as Mr. Albemarle was, disposed to be frightened of all things in a barnyard. Mr. Albemarle was not similarly afraid of a wild animal, but all things in a barnyard had been husbanded there by a human malfeasant who wore wellies and had relations with the things in the barnyard, which consequently would bite you or kick you or step on you when they could. The slapped alien stood next to Mr. Albemarle with a gleam in his eye and had a lip-smacking expression, if a lip-smacking expression can be had by a party without, apparently, any lips. As he had with the photographer and the turkey, Mr. Albemarle held his ground, standing erect and turning ever so slightly askance to the alien so there would not be a clean, open shot to his private parts if it came to that.

It came to that. No sooner had he thought of that turkey the size of a tumbleweed in its waist-high dirty feathers gazing with its evil scaly wattled head at his crotch than the alien of affection touched him there very lightly and very quickly with a flipper. "Hey!" Mr. Albemarle said.

"Just a reading, old man," said the alien. "No fun intended."

"What's a reading?"

"We read your affinity for affection," the first alien said to Mr. Albemarle. Of the second alien he asked, "What's he look like?"

"Twisted."

Mr. Albemarle adjusted himself subtly in his pants and turned a little more askance from the alien who had touched him. "What do you mean, *twisted*?"

"The worm of your passion," the first alien said, "is twisted."

"Well, it straightens out," Mr. Albemarle said.

"No," the alien said. "*You* straighten out, sir, as Johnny Carson once elicited from Mrs. Arnold Palmer that she straightens out Mr. Arnold Palmer's putter by kissing his balls. *You* straighten out, sir, but the worm of your passion is twisted."

"Your desire, in other words," the second alien said, now a respectful distance from him, "is not clean and open but dirty and veiled. Something untoward happened to you at a delicate moment in the opening of the petals of your heart—"

"Shut up," the first alien said. "Excuse him," he said to Mr. Albemarle. "He tends to make jokes when he should not. We are safer in not speaking of flowers. We are safer in speaking of worms. And the worm of your passion is twisted, bent, kinked, and not, as it should be, straight, straight, and straight."

"Is this bad?"

"It is bad, yes, but you are not alone. Only one person on earth we've checked out is straight. That's Pat Boone."

"Everybody else is . . . twisted?"

"More or less. You are more than less."

The second alien, who had taken the actual reading, said, "Lucky you're alive, man. It's like a Grand Prix course down there."

"What he means, sir," the first alien said, "is that before the engine of your desire crosses the finish line it must negotiate a tortuous course and use the transmission to preserve the brakes and discard and remount many new tires and—"

"Hey!" It was the second alien waving them over to the edge of the wall. There all the other aliens were, peering down.

"Can you guys see down there?" Mr. Albemarle asked. "Take a reading?"

The aliens of affection were whistling to themselves in amazement. "Never seen the like of it." "That is *bizarre*." "Takes the effing cake."

"What is it?"

"Nothing, man," one of them said.

"Nothing? Don't *nothing, man* me, sir. I patrol the watchtower and have every right to know what is down there."

The aliens went on marveling at whatever it was they could see or detect in the moat, if it was a moat. Mr. Albemarle looked in appeal to the first, apparently chief, alien, who pulled him aside.

"We've encountered the odd thing of the heart in our job," he told Mr. Albemarle.

"What's down there?" Mr. Albemarle observed the alien in apparent consideration of whether, and how, to tell him.

"I'm in *charge* here," Mr. Albemarle said. "Need to know." He'd always liked that phrase: we'll keep you on a need-to-know basis, so when they torture you, you will only be on a need-to-be-beat basis for so long.

"Broken hearts," the alien said.

"Sir?"

"About four million broken hearts down there, scrap hearts, badly deteriorated, cut you to ribbons before you hit the water."

"Not crocodiles or bicycles?"

At this the alien started laughing. The other aliens came over to see what was funny.

"What?" they said. The alien laughed even harder and refused to tell. They began goosing him with their flippers, trying to tickle it out of him, Mr. Albemarle supposed. Mr. Albemarle became embarrassed. He had said something, it was clear, ridiculous. But a moment ago, crocodiles on the one hand and bicycles on the other had made sense.

"I said crocodiles or bicycles," Mr. Albemarle told them. "I thought it was crocodiles down there, and some sodiers thought it was old bicycles."

The group of aliens politely tried to contain its mirth. The slapped alien generously came up to Mr. Albemarle and comforted him. "Understandable, man. No way you could know. We've never heard of it ourselves."

"I don't even know what I'm *doing* out here, all along the watchtower," Mr. Albemarle said. "Let alone what's in a goddamn moat I can't even see."

"Well, buddy," said the slapped alien, to whom Mr. Albemarle felt the most affinity (and he hoped it wasn't because this alien had touched lightly and quickly his crotch), "you know what you are doing now. You are watching over a giant spoilbank of broken hearts."

"My God. Still, what do I *do*?"

"Not sure on that. We break them. We are not concerned with their repair or storage. It would appear that these hearts here have been, in Navy parlance, mothballed. It appears you are simply to *watch* them."

"Watch all the broken hearts, all along the watchtower."

"Yes."

"In the world."

"Yes."

"And mine—it's broken too?"

"The worm of your passion is twisted, sir. Your heart is up here on the watchtower, not altogether broken. We have no orders to break hearts. We merely alienate affection. The broken heart is, you might say, collateral damage."

"I have mismanaged my affections."

"That you have, sir. In spades. We have no orders to further alienate your affections. The reading we took of you was casual, informational only, whimsical."

"The worm of my passion is twisted?"

"Twisted badly, sir. But the worm is alive."

"Is that good?"

"Depends, sir, on your outlook. Are you an absolutist or a relativist, ideal or practical in your worldly posture?"

"I am a muddle of—"

"Muddlers, sir, do not go unpunished. The moat is filled with muddlers."

At this Mr. Albemarle peered over the edge of the wall, frightened and yet oddly buoyed up by this talk. He was a twisted muddler but not (yet) down there on the spoilbank of the broken. It gave him a sudden hankering to have his hair cut in a barbershop where they'd put sweet-smelling talc and tonic on his shaved neck and let him chew Juicy Fruit in the chair. He could chew fresh Juicy Fruit after the haircut walking down the street in the sun with his perfumed head gleaming in the sun. He could find a girlfriend and try it again.

"Hey!" he said to the aliens. "If you guys . . . I mean, do you guys have any plans for me? Am I on the list?"

"No. You're singing the blues already, sir."

"Okay."

In a flurry of salutes and waves—Mr. Albemarle did not want to shake hands with the flippers, and the aliens did not actually offer them—the aliens were gone.

When the sodiers and aliens had left him alone, patrolling all along the watchtower better informed of his mission and better equipped for it, Mr. Albemarle felt momentarily better. He had that new-haircut sweet air about him and felt he was wearing new clothes, and he stepped lightly and lively all along the watchtower.

But soon the drug put in him by the sodiers and the aliens wore off. The gear began to seem a rather *Sodier of Fortune* aggregation of pot metal and fish dye and it was clanky and in the way. He discarded it in a neat pile.

What the aliens had given him was worse: the worm of his passion was twisted. This news, coupled with the revelations about the moat of hearts and about their having no call to further alienate his own affections, had calmed Mr. Albemarle when the penguinesque aliens of affection had been present. But now that they were gone he was nervous. It was like, he supposed, turning yourself in to the doctor during illness; you were still sick as a dog, but the mere presence of a man in charge of that in a lab coat and in an ethyl-alcohol atmosphere suggested your troubles would soon be over.

Now Mr. Albemarle realized the aliens had given him no such assurance. They had said in fact he was too alienated in his affections already for them to bother with alienating them further, which was not unlike being deemed terminal by the good doctor.

At first the aliens' pronouncing "The worm of your passion is twisted" had had an oddly calming, if not outright narcotic, effect on Mr. Albemarle. *That explains everything!* was what he had thought. Now he thought it explained nothing, and where it had calmed him it frightened him. "The worm of my passion is twisted," he said to himself, and aloud over the moat, and all along the watchtower, feeling worse and worse and worse. "The worm of my passion is twisted."

Mr. Albemarle then had a vision of his genitals twisted into knots. This was oddly comforting, also. It did not bother him. He chuckled, in fact, at the idea, and he recalled a woman once at a cocktail party declaiming to people whom she thought interested but who were not, "My husband's genitals are like knotted rope." Everyone had left her and gone over to talk with her husband in sympathetic moods.

Mr. Albemarle knew that the aliens meant something deeper and worse, as they had told him, and that they were right. His passion was bent and his desire was dirty and veiled. He knew men whose passion was straightforward and whose desire was clean and open and who were not Pat Boone. They were true cowboys of the heart. They saw what they wanted (and knew it), they asked for it, and when they got it they sang praise around the campfire in a clear voice and got up early and made coffee for it and kissed it and hit the trail, the happy trail, until nightfall and bedfall and bliss. These cowboys had cowgirls: open-eyed girls in red skirts who danced with you if you asked and kissed you back if you waited long enough to kiss them first. And a true cowboy knew how to wait, and he knew whom to kiss in the first place.

Mr. Albemarle did not know whom to kiss because he wanted to kiss no one, really, and when he got tired of that he wanted to kiss everyone. At that point, waiting seemed contraindicated. Waiting for what? For *everyone* to say yes? It was ridiculous. He had the image of a real cowboy of the heart, his passion straight and clean and open, sitting a bull in the chute, packing his hand in the harness very carefully and taking a long time while the bull snorted and farted and stomped and fumed and flared, giving the word when he was ready, and in a happy breeze of preparedness blasting into danger and waving for balance astride it for a regulation period and vaulting into the air and landing on two feet and walking proudly across the sand to receive his score, with which, good or bad, he would be content.

By contrast, Mr. Albemarle would not deign get on the bull until the last minute, and then would disdainfully sit sidesaddle on it and it would erupt and the rest would be an ignominious confusion of injuries and clowns coming to his rescue. That is what "the worm of your passion is twisted" meant. It meant not a ride and a score but injury and clowns holding your hand.

Mr. Albemarle walked all along the watchtower, whistling gloomily and studying the clouds. He imagined the hearts in the moat — the aliens had said a spoilbank of hearts — in great cumulus piles, great billowy stacks of puffy, shifting, vaporous grief, under the still water.

He cupped his mouth and in a low, smooth, strong voice intoned to the moat:

"Cawboy to moat, cawboy to spoils of love —

"What am I going to do with myself, now that I know it

to be useless? I am tenebrous, or tenebrious if you prefer, it's all the same. When the big bulldog get in trouble, puppy-dog britches will fit him fine."

The water, or whatever was actually down there, remained still.

On his next morning's patrol, which he went about naked, having liked the sensation of discarding all the sodiers' gear and not seeing the logical end to discarding things, he met a woman on the wall. This is the way it is in life, he reflected; when you go naked, for once, you run into somebody you might prefer not see you naked. There was a woman not fifty yards ahead and Mr. Albemarle at least had the gumption to keep going, not to run. His nakedness if anything emboldened his step, martialized it a bit, so that by the time he actually came up to her he was in a subdued goose step and was looking perfectly natural about it.

"Hey, *cawboy*," she said with a leer. "I been hearing you sing the blues up here all the livelong day." This testiness was coming out of an otherwise happy, innocent-looking woman reminiscent of Dale Evans. She had on the red skirt that Mr. Albemarle had pictured when he was taking inventory regarding straight desire and twisted desire. The red skirt flared out wide and short and had a modest but sexy fringe on it. It allowed you to see where the leg of the wearer began to be the butt of the wearer, and it gave the onlooker pause and a kind of stillborn gulp.

He was looking at this Dale Evans in her skirt saying this contradictory Mae West stuff to him, naked and in the arrested gulp and not now looking at the skirt or the legs or the legs grading into the butt, actually there was nothing gradual about it—

"Cawboy," Dale Mae was saying, "I want you to sing me some o' them blues."

"I don't sing," Mr. Albemarle said.

"Yesterday you sang:
'When the big bulldog in trouble
Puppy-dog britches fit him fine.'

You sang this in a clear campfire voice that lulled the cows and woke me up. I been sleepin' a long long long long long long time."

"That sounds like a long time," Mr. Albemarle said, stupidly, desperately trying to calculate how she heard him, where she was or had been to hear him singing to the moat. *In the moat?*

"Are you from the spoilbank of broken hearts?"

"The what?"

"The moat?"

"The what?"

"Is your heart broken?"

Dale Mae looked at him as if she had noticed for the first time he was naked, or as if he had lost his mind, which was, he considered, the same look. "Why don't you get dressed so we can dance," Dale Mae said. "Put on some of that Soldier of Fortune shit in a pile over there."

"*Sodier* of Fortune," Mr. Albemarle corrected, liking her. He fairly skipped over to the military paraphernalia and slapped on a quantity of it and stood almost breathless before Dale Mae in her flared red skirt and delicious fringe, ready to dance, or whatever.

"I warn you," he said. "I put you on notice right now. I have . . . the worm of my passion is twisted."

"It better be," Dale Mae said.

"By all assurances, it is *badly* twisted."

"When the big bulldog get in trouble, he should turn on some music and dance," Dale Mae said. "Take this bitch in hand, sir, and fret not your twisted passion."

"Yes, ma'am."

Mr. Albemarle did as he was told. All along the watchtower, they danced. It was a stepless but not beatless dance, hip to hip, pocket to bone, thrust to hollow. Gradually Dale Mae swatted away the annoying military hardware and left Mr. Albemarle as elegant as Fred Astaire, and gradually she herself softened and melted and fairly oozed into his arms, and they made in their heads plans to remain together and untwist Mr. Albemarle's passion and to do to Dale Mae's passion whatever in the way of no harm could yet be done to it. Dale Mae had a beauty mark on her cheek, which Mr. Albemarle admired until he touched it and it came off on his finger and appeared to be a piece of insect and he flicked it over the wall and thought no more of it and admired without impediment the dreamy, relaxed face of Dale Mae who had come to him unbidden and unhesitant and unheeding of certain dangers. This gave him a good feeling and made his puppy-dog britches fit him a little less fine. He was bulldog big enough already to kiss this cowgirl on the neck.

"Sugar," Dale Mae said, "it's the hardest thing to remember. All I can be is me, and all you can be is you."

"What's that mean?"

"I have no idea. Sing me some of them blues."

Mr. Albemarle sang:

"What I like about roses I like a lot —
I like a smell, a thorn, that jungle rot.
I like a red, a yeller, a vulvate pink.
And a king bee going down the drink."

Mr. Albemarle and Dale Mae got themselves some coffee and got naked and got squared away for some intimate quality time together in a small bungalow he'd found in the fog, which intimate quality time Mr. Albemarle kicked off by announcing to Dale Mae, sitting cross-legged on the bed with her coffee steaming her breasts and looking to Mr. Albemarle some deliciously beautiful, perfectly joined in her parts and the parts appearing to be cream and vanilla and cinnamon and cherry and chocolate, and some of her looked like bread, also, smooth tender bread like host wafers — he tore himself away and said, "I warn you, I'm a bad piece of work, emotionally."

"Well bully for you," Dale Mae said. "Do you know what to do *with me*?"

"I believe I do," Mr. Albemarle said, gently placing a knee on the bed and taking Dale Mae's coffee and setting it safely on a night table so she did not get burned in the clapping straits of his desire. He clapped onto her like an honest man.

She returned everything he gave her by time and a half. It knocked him silly and made him pat his own butt, looking for his wallet, when it was over. He did this when he wasn't sure who he was. In the willing arms of an agreeable woman possessed of reason and courage, Mr. Albemarle had to doubt it could really be him she was holding and he wanted invariably at these moments to see his wallet.

"Relax, you piece of work," Dale Mae said.

"Okay."

He did. It was difficult, to do that. Relaxing was hard, and dangerous, he did not trust it. That was why you had drunks. They had the most difficulty relaxing. They wanted it most, feared it most, claimed it most, almost never managed it.

"I will break your heart," he said to Dale Mae, breathing hard on her breast, a sugary warm air coming from it as if it were a lobe of a radiator.

"Hmmm?" Dale Mae asked. "You go right ahead."

"Go ahead?"

"Why not? Break break break."

Some day, maybe today, he was going to do a woman right. Dale Mae's breast was next to his eye and looked like a cake with one of those high-speed-photo milk-drop crowns on it. He had a tear in his eye and was hungry for cake. It was *thanklessness* that plagued and dogged hard the heels of affection. Affection was that which, and the only thing on earth which, you should be eternally thankful for.

When Mr. Albemarle got up from these his exertions upon Dale Mae the warm giving stranger, he felt fresh and sweet as a large piece of peppermint candy. He told Dale Mae this and she told him he'd better take a shower, then, and get over it. He kissed her and she kissed back and he took the shower and she was still there when he got out. Her heart hadn't been broken yet. It was progress. There was hope.

"It's not easy," Mr. Albemarle said later when they were strolling all along the watchtower hand in hand and in love, "to work this particular bit of magic."

"What particular bit of magic?" Dale Mae asked.

"Marriage."

"Indeed," Dale Mae said, noticing a piece of shale on the walk and throwing it over the edge. Mr. Albemarle waited to hear it land, curious he had never tried a sounding in the mysterious moat before. He was still keening his ear when Dale Mae said, "*This* particular bit of magic? You deem us *married?*"

"In a figure of—"

"In a figure of nothing. Not speech, not nothing."

"*Okay*. Sheesh! What's up your reconnaissance butt?"

"My what?"

"*Nothing*."

He held her hand, petulantly but not unhappily. Marriage *was* a tricky bit of magic. Holding hands was a tricky bit of magic. She needn't be so hyper. There were—it occurred to him, now having been posted to the old verity that he was, whether holding hands or married or not, finally alone, always—there were people who had in their minds something called "a true marriage," as opposed, Mr. Albemarle supposed, to a *pro forma* marriage. He had no idea what this true marriage purported to be. He was not speaking of it when he constructed his pithy impertinence about magic and a marriage being made to work. He meant the false kind. It was a tricky bit of magic to *stay together*, was what he meant.

"I meant, it's a tricky bit of magic to *stay together*," he now said to Dale Mae, who squeezed his hand and patted their held hands with her free one as if to say, "You'll be all right." This little gesture proved his point: it was condescending enough that he wanted to take his hand back.

But she was, of course, right. Magic or not, tricky or not, it would bear no comment, it needed no more pressure upon it, the gratuitous happy union, than was naturally on it, the meeting and clinging together of two naturally repellent, irregular surfaces. They clung together out of desire but were aided, in his view, in their sticking together by a sap of hurt. This glue oozed from them despite themselves. For all Dale Mae's tough rightness, she was holding hands too. She was very tough and very soft. She was nougat.

"You're a nougat," Mr. Albemarle said to her, announcing it at large all along the watchtower. Emboldened, he then said, a little less broadly, a little more conspiratorially, "True marriage schmoo schmarriage."

"What?"

"Schmoo schmarriage," he repeated.

Dale Mae thumped him on the nose and held him by the back of the neck with one hand and at the small of the back with the other and pulled hard with both hands, scaring him with her strength.

All along the watchtower, it was quiet. "I think songbirds are overrated," Mr. Albemarle offered. "Really inflated. Not nowhere *near* what they're cracked up to be."

Mr. Albemarle got them two buckets of range balls from a vending machine he'd never seen all along the watchtower before. As much as he had patrolled it, this caused him wonder. The machine itself was a wonder: a plastic fluorescent box dispensing not junk food or soda water but golf balls. What would come out of a vending machine next? Shoes? Pets? Beside the machine, incongruously to his mind, was a barrel full of clubs, for free use in ridding yourself of your buckets of balls. Mr. Albemarle got them each a driver, and he and Dale Mae slapped and topped and scuffed and hooked and sliced and shanked and chillied the balls into the moat of spoiled affection. Mr. Albemarle had the feeling that each ball contained a message of some sort to the brokenhearted from the not yet broken. They were like fortune cookies except that they were more like misfortune cookies. He could not imagine what one of these misfortunes might actually have said, and when he inspected a ball it read only *Pro-staff* or *Titleist 4* or *The Golden Bear*. Yet he felt that each ball, whether it soared over or squibbed immediately down into the moat, carried a secret meaning from the players all along the watchtower to the wrecked players beneath it.

They had a good time. Each ball was a small celebration of their gratuitous, so far successful affection above the moat of moping: each ball said, "Here, you sad sacks, *here*." They were probably, in their hand-holding glee and innocent kissing mirth, only minutes away from hurling themselves like badly hit balls themselves down into their broken brethren, but for the moment they felt fine and superior, lucky and happy, the way a new couple is supposed to feel.

Mr. Albemarle addressed each ball with a little wiggle of his butt and hands, a steadying sigh, *arm straight, head down, slow uptake, pause, how long will it be before she and I are back to normal, at each other instead of on*, whap! ball going God knows where, anywhere but straight. Mr. Albemarle could somehow induce a golf ball to wind up *behind* him. Dale Mae, in her red, fringed skirt, the fringes snapping like tiny whips when she cracked a ball into the ozone of ruined love before them, did better: her balls went forward.

That's how it is with women, Mr. Albemarle thought. They want forward, they get forward. Not so with me, which is where all the bluster obtains. *Talk* forward if you achieve backward. Bluster and cheer, the man's ticket to the prom. Bluster and cheer take reason and balls to the dance of life, and it goes reasonably well as long as the corsage is fresh. Then reason divorces cheer, and balls beat bluster, and the long diurnal haul to mildew of the heart is on. Mr. Albemarle teed up an X-out and hit it, smiling, best he could.

When they got back from the range, such as it was—the glowing ball dispenser, the ball baskets like Amazon brassieres, the clubs on the honor system—they prepared to frolic naked. Mr. Albemarle dropped his wallet on a chair beside the bed and out the corner of his eyes saw the wallet move. "Look," Dale Mae said, "there's a lizard."

There was a lizard coming out of Mr. Albemarle's wallet. It was nearly the color of the dollar bills from which it emerged, its head made quick birdlike assessments of the situation, and it ran.

"What *was* that?" Mr. Albemarle asked.

"That was Elvis," Dale Mae said, "in a green one-dollar cape. *Get in the bed*."

Mr. Albemarle did as he was told.

There is much to be said for doing as one is told. Mr. Albemarle had come to see life as a parabola of sorts plotted over time against doing and not doing as one is told. Roughly, infancy and maturity were close to a baseline of obeying what others expected of you, and puberty and its aftermath, which was a variable period, took you on the upward part of the bell-like curve away from the baseline of doing what you were told. You soared on a roller-coaster hump of doing *not* what you were told and it felt good but finally your stomach got a bit light and uneasy and you started, through natural forces and not reluctantly, to come back down toward agreeability. Having ridden around with your hands off the bar and screaming, you were now willing—it was even exhilarating—to do precisely as you were told. It was fun in fact to subvert the voice telling you what to do a little by being instantly agreeable, by even anticipating instructions. This was pulling the wool on the bourgeois.

This was one reason Mr. Albemarle did not object to his current job, walking all along the watchtower. He yet had no good idea what he was doing, despite the large assurances and hints supplied him by the aliens of affection, but he found doing it agreeable because he had apparently been, however mysteriously, told to do it. So he did it. Living well was not the best revenge; doing exactly what you are told is the best revenge. The blame or fault in your doing it, if any obtains, rests upon those telling you what to do. The masses of folk going over cliffs in the name of this or that religion were onto the beauty of this revenge, but Mr. Albemarle liked the less obvious vengeance of obeying the smallest whim, the fine print of commandments that were issuing like radio signals from everyone and everything around him, from the very fabric of civilized life. From utter strangers on the street, to foreign governments, everyone had ideas about what you were supposed to do. Your job, as baseline parabola wire walker, was to divine their (sometimes tacit) wishes and appear to obey them. This is what civilized human life boiled down to.

Animals, Mr. Albemarle had noticed, and it was not surprising, were immune. They could not hear the radio. They heard only their "instincts," which excused all their nasty behavior. Periodically an animal would be trained—i.e., forced to listen to the radio. Animal trainers were, ironically, those most wont on earth to speak of human freedom, iconoclasm, nonconformity as *summae bonae*. And they were, appropriately, dirtier than most people, unruly, outspoken in hard-to-follow ways, united beyond these traits in their insistence that tuning in a horse or a bear or a dog to hear the radio of doing what it was told somehow increased *its* freedom. These notions gave Mr. Albemarle the idea of opening an obedience school for dogs all along the watchtower. He would train all the dogs all along the watchtower to leap into the moat and become brokenhearted-man's best friend. He liked this idea very much. Training a dog to leap into space would be a test, probably, but it would be imminently possible if you weren't soft-headed. The larger problem with the idea was that he hadn't seen a dog in all his days all along the watchtower.

When Dale Mae woke up, looking ravishing, he said to her, "Do you think we need a dog?" She said, "I don't think we *need* a dog."

That was that.

"I'm like one of those Iroquois steel workers," Mr. Albemarle said. "I just naturally put one foot down in front of the other, straight, without looking down, all along the watchtower whether there are dogs on it or not and all along the parabola of doing what I'm told. I can walk that line as steady as Ricky Wallenda on a wire, but no leapfrog."

"No leapfrog?"

"No leapfrog. Ricky Wallenda quit leapfrog. He fell doing leapfrog."

"I see."

"Just do what you're told, but no leapfrog."

"I see."

The amazing thing about Dale Mae, about any tough woman who could still smile after enduring her own time on the parabola of doing and not doing as she was told, was that she *did* see. They could see right through a fog of nonsense to the rock or reef behind it. They'd abandoned radar in favor of a finger in the wind. This is why men liked them and were driven crazy by them. Men were content with a finger in the wind only when they were defeated or tired. Women used a finger in the wind cinching victory first thing in the morning. Without women, men would be giant raw quivering analytical anuses. Mr. Albemarle was comforted by this summation he had formulated and went to sleep on Dale Mae's bosom.

Mr. Albemarle found a writing desk all along the watchtower and stationery inside it so sat down to write a letter. "Take a letter," he said to himself and by way of sexual harassment palmed his own butt and sat down.

Dear [blank; he couldn't determine whom to write],
I know you think ill of me. That is because I am weak and mean. But keep in mind that . . . [here he faltered] . . . that . . . [he could think of nothing now in his behalf, in his defense, to say to the person or persons whom he could not think of either] . . .
Love,
Troy

Troy was not his name, nor did he want to assume it. He looked the letter over and liked it. It summed up his position nicely. It was all you could say if the worm of your passion was twisted, your affections were all mismanaged and *always would be*. "Keep in mind that . . . that . . ." that nothing. *Love, Troy*. Did he mean the city, the myth of epic war over an impossibly beautiful woman? Who cared.

He decided to make a thousand copies of the letter and somehow devise a mailing list that would be appropriate and have mailing labels applied by a machine so the entire affair would not be labor-intensive and he wouldn't have to lick a thousand stamps and write addresses and harass himself further. The sexual harassment of one's own self was the most insidious form of sexual harassment and there was to his knowledge no legal protection against it.

That want seemed a huge oversight on the part of the stewards of modern civilized life who had turned life into injury and redress, loss and litigation. The final moment in it all would be every citizen suing himself or herself for damages resulting from his or her own excesses and negligences with respect to himself or herself and his or her personal aggrandizement or lack thereof. The vista of the denizens of the modern world suing themselves into bankruptcy gave hope where there had not been any. This was a beautiful prospect to Mr. Albemarle, patrolling all along the watchtower—a kind of global legal self-immolation that would leave a few survivors who bore no one else and themselves no ill will. He suddenly felt, in possession of this vision, that he might be a prophet of some sort: the elect, here all along the watchtower not to guard a moat of the brokenhearted but to witness a Trojan War of tortes. He was going to observe World War III, which was going to be a global litigious meltdown, from a safe purchase on his lawless wall.

Mr. Albemarle left the letter on top of the writing desk with instructions for its copying and mailing to one thousand appropriate parties, TBA. He had no idea whom the instructions were for, but if someone came along and assumed the duty it would be better than if someone didn't. Leaving the desk he noticed a phone booth he had never seen before and stepped in it and dialed a number.
"Hello?"
"Hello. Good, it's you."
"Who is this?"
"Troy Albemarle."
"Who?"
"I don't know. I just wanted to tell you that I'm lonely."
"You have the wrong number."
"No, I don't."
"You don't? You don't know me and I don't know you."
"You're a *woman*," Mr. Albemarle said, with more force than he intended, "and I just wanted to tell you that I'm lonely."

"Look, mister. That's what you tell your *own* woman, not a stranger."

"Look, yourself. If I tell my *own* woman I'm lonely, she'll think me silly."

"Maybe you are."

"Maybe I am. I don't dispute it. But to accede that one is silly is not to deny that one is lonely."

"It probably accounts for it."

"It *probably does!*" Mr. Albemarle all but shouted, slamming the phone into its chrome, spring-loaded cradle, fully satisfied.

When he saw Dale Mae, approaching with a shotgun, he thought to test the wisdom of the conversation with the strange woman, with whom he was in love.

"Dale Mae, I'm lonely."

"Don't be silly," Dale Mae said.

"Yes!"

"What's the matter with you?"

"Nothing."

"Do you want to shoot some skeet?"

"Of course I want to shoot some skeet."

"Well, come on. There's a skeet range down the way."

"I never saw a *skeet range* all along the watchtower," Mr. Albemarle said. "A *lot* of things, actually, are—"

"Come on, lonely heart. My daddy taught me one thing and I'm going to show you what it is."

"Do, do, do," Mr. Albemarle said, taking a look around for the presence of witnesses to this exchange. There were none that he could see, which, he knew, meant not much. *Nothing apparent* meant more, in these days, than *something obvious*. He was getting used to that. It took some doing, but he was doing it.

The skeet range was of the nothing-apparent type. Dale Mae stopped walking, put two shells in her gun and crisply closed it, looking dreamy-eyed at Mr. Albemarle and patting the gun and saying of it "Parker" in the lowest, sexiest voice he'd ever heard, and then her eyes cleared and she turned to face the void beyond the wall, said "Pull," and blew to infinitely small pieces a thing which seemed to fly from the front face of the wall. It looked like a 45 rpm record before she hit it; Mr. Albemarle concluded it had been a clay skeet after she hit it. She kept saying "Pull" and blasting that which flew, left right high low, to bits, and she took a long, lusty snort of the thick cordite smell in the air and scuffed some of the wadding from her shells off the wall and said, "Mone get me some iced tea and fried chicken when I get through shooting, and then kiss you to death," and resumed firing, shooting backwards and between her legs and one-handed from the hip, like a gunslinger with a three-foot-long pistol, *missing nothing*, and Mr. Albemarle started talking, uncontrollably, agreeably:

"In the first grade had a teach name Mrs. Campbell that was the end of sweetness for me in the, ah, official realm. Next year ozone, I mean second grade in orange groves, etc. Mother had water break and taxi to hospital, golf-course father, had swimming lessons chlorine nose. A siege of masturbation ensued. Declined professional life—had *choice*, too. Somehow at juncture early in life where you elect to watch birds or not I deigned not. *Fuck birds*. This is sad. I am holy in my disregard of the holy. Sitting upright in a Studebaker or some other classically lined failure is the attitude in which I see myself for a final portrait in the yearbook of life. Depth charges *look* like 55-gallon drums but I suspect they are really not that innocent-looking up close. Reservations at hotels and restaurants and airlines are for—" he stopped and snorted lustily the cordite himself and realized he had been aping Dale Mae's shooting in mime. He looked like a fool. She kept shooting. She was a one-person firefight. She would fill the moat with clay shards and wads.

"I want the certainty of uncertainty. I declare nothing to customs, ever. Transgressions of a social and moral sort interest me: philosophically I mean. They assume—I mean those *who* assume to know a transgression—that the points A and B for the gression to trans are known. I've had trouble, since the ozone of second grade and the chlorine and my mother holding herself, having peed in her pants and cursing my father, and since the large beautiful hognose snake I was too scared of to pick up in the orange grove so went home to get a jar to invite him to crawl into, which took about a half hour and, well, the snake didn't wait around, I've had trouble knowing point A and point B in order to correctly perceive, or conceive, transgression."

"Let's go get some chicken," Dale Mae said.

"That sounds delicious. That sounds good. That sounds not urbane but divine anyway—"

"Shut up, baby. I can't kiss you, you go off your rocker."

"You shoot that gun I shoot my mouth, is all. I—"

There was, not improbably, tea and fried chicken in a handsome woven basket, and a red-checkered tablecloth for them to have the picnic on, all along the watchtower.

Selling hot, melted ice cream from a rolling cart, like soup, or to put on pastries, or something, he supposed, Mr. Albemarle pushed an umbrellaed cart all along the watchtower. It had four rather small wheels instead of the more conventional two large wheels used by food vendors, and they flibbered and squalled, drawing his attention away from trying to figure whose idea it was to try to sell hot ice cream to pondering how much of life, finally, was pushing things around on wheels. The sick were flibbering and squalling down halls of disinfectant, the healthy down freeways of octane, dessert in a good restaurant flibbered and squalled up to you in a cart much like his—if the human race had gone as mad for fire as it had for the wheel, the earth would be a black cinder. Instead it was a scarred, runover thing, tracks all over it, resembling in the long view one of those world's largest balls of twine, in this case one as large *as* the world.

Dale Mae was down the way and Mr. Albemarle moved along the way. Who was going to buy hot ice cream? Who, all along the watchtower, was going to buy anything? There *was* no one all along the watchtower, so far, except the sodiers, the aliens of affection, and now Dale Mae. Mr. Albemarle looked around to see if perchance anyone was watching and pushed the cart of bubbling ice cream—it smelled cloyingly sweet—over the edge of the watchtower into the moat, brushing his hands together briskly as if he'd handily completed a nasty task. He whistled a happy tune, one that appeared to be random notes, and sauntered all along the watchtower.

Mr. Albemarle stopped his whistling and sauntering in midblow and midstep. He had an old-fashioned crisis. He was suddenly transfixed by one of the old human antiverities: he had *no idea what he was doing, or was supposed to do.* Pal with sodiers, let aliens of affection feel you up, romp with a Dale Mae, push boiling ice cream into a moat—these things you did in life because they came along. You did them. You even did them well, if you cared to—Dale Mae said the worm of his passion was *exquisitely* twisted. But so what? What of it? What *then*? What *now*? What *point*?

He stood there feeling slump-shouldered and low. He had a vision of a different kind of life. There were men who, say, ran car dealerships and bought acreage and had their friends out to shoot quail and they all drank out of these Old-Fashioned glasses with pheasants painted on them, painted "by hand" it said in the expensive mail-order catalogue the car-dealer quail-shooter's wife ordered the glasses out of. The wife and the other wives were in the kitchen discussing what the wives of car dealers and bankers and brokers discuss. They were wearing pleated Bermuda shorts and none of them was too fat. The men were content with them, even loved them, and did not have affairs too much. The men laughed easily among themselves at things that were not too funny. Mr. Albemarle was outside this, all of this.

He knew that were he inside it, the point-of-life problem might not be resolved, but he knew it would not, if he were drinking Wild Turkey and talking Republican politics, come up. From his vantage and distance, quail glasses and okaying the deficit might well be *exactly* the point of life, he could not tell. But he was certain that he—all along the watchtower, with (accidentally) a woman who could (incidentally) shoot the quail but who would (certainly) shoot the quail glasses also—was never going to get the point. He was, he realized, standing there looking at the ball. He did not see that it helped anything. If you paused to look at the ball you were going to be tackled for no gain, or for a loss; whereas if you just at least *ran*, you stood a chance of gaining yardage. That you had no idea what a yard meant was no argument to lose yardage, or was it? How had he gotten to walking all along the watchtower? Was it not a losing of yardage? Was being on the watchtower with a woman who could probably shoot the painted quail off a glass without breaking the glass not somehow the negative image of life on the plantation, where the plantation had nothing planted on it but feed for the birds who would be painted on the glasses lovingly held and admired as symbols of the good life? At this cerebration Mr. Albemarle was forced to sit down and say, "Whew!" He'd had, he thought, some kind of epiphany. "Whew!" he said again. It helped.

"What's wrong with you?" Dale Mae said, scaring him. He'd not heard her come up. He wondered if the watchtower were getting softer, or something.

"Nothing," he said. "If I threw a hand-painted quail glass in the air, could you shoot the paint off it without breaking the glass?"

"Do it all the time," Dale Mae said. "Problem is catching the glass. That's hard. Usually you get you a party of car dealers and brokers to shag 'em. Out there in their Filson pants and Barbour coats, pumping hell-for-leather through the gorse, flushing actual quail. There are ironies."

Mr. Albemarle looked at her hard. Either she was demonic and had possessed his brain, or something else of a weird and too intimate nature was going on.

"Where are the wives?" he asked.
"What wives?"
"To the glass catchers."
"In the kitchen with Dinah strummin' on the old banjo."
"Thought so."
"Let's get us some ice cream."
"Can't."
"Why not?"
"I rolled the cart into the moat."
"You *what*?"

"Well, it was *boiled* ice cream. Did you want *boiled* ice cream?"

"No. I want hard cold ice cream."

"Me too."

Like that, they were together, hand in hand, strolling all along the watchtower looking for ice cream proper, Mr. Albemarle's epiphany behind him.

They walked by the writing desk where Mr. Albemarle had left instructions for the phantom secretary to mail his one thousand letters it seemed just seconds before, and the desk was covered in vines. He remarked on it to Dale Mae.

"Heart mildew," Dale Mae said.

"What's that?"

"It's what grows on sites of affection. If you'd left that desk alone, or left a real letter on it that was to be mailed to one thousand people for whom you never had or expected to have affection, there'd be no vine on it. Your letter, lame-o one that it is, brings on the jungle. Am I on that mailing list?"

"Not yet. I only have the brokenhearted on that list."

"A thousand?"

"Well, I rounded up."

"As well you might. As well might we all. It is a proposition of such close tolerances, at least before the parts are worn out from friction, that pairing a thousand bolts to a thousand nuts does not seem excessive. Consider thread count, mismatched metals—"

"Dale Mae, could we talk about something else?"

"Sure, baby. What?"

"I once threw away a Craftsman circular saw when all that was wrong with it was a broken tooth on a drive gear. This, the whole-thing throwing away, was a waste. I regret it. That whole saw—motor, blade, and all—in a plastic garbage bag, now in a landfill, I guess, with its bad gear nearby somewhere in the great noncomposting amalgam of jetsam, if you have jetsam on land, or flotsam, I don't know the difference, but anyway it, the saw, in its exploded view (I did not reassemble it) is packed into some clayey sand with whatever else I threw away with it and whatever else other people threw away that day and there are seagulls flying overhead so maybe it's fair to call the saw flotsam, or jetsam, where you have gulls you have salvage, just as where you have smoke you have fire."

"Is that it?" Dale Mae asked.

"No. That is the tip of the lettuce. I once took four baby cardinals from their nest in a relocation program of my own devising. They, the hairless little blue pterodactyls, were to be moved to a 'safer' place, God knows where. For this transport they were placed on a wooden paddle of the sort you are to strike a rubber ball with repeatedly as it returns to the paddle via an elastic band. I have blocked the name of the toy."

"Fly Back," Dale Mae said.

"The birds," Mr. Albemarle said, "peeping and squalling, were red-skinned and blue-blooded underneath the fine cactusey down on them, giving them a purple scrotal texture until they fell off into an ant bed. The kind of squirming they did, which made me unable (afraid) to cup them on the paddle, did not look radically different from the kind of writhing they did once they fell off and the ants were on them, but it was. They writhed to death, the baby cardinals, right there at my feet, at the foot of the tree in which their erstwhile happy safe home sat empty but for the hysterical parents flitting in and out. Right there at my feet, except I slunk my feet off somewhere to contemplate what went wrong, how the little bastards should have known better than to *scare me* like that."

"Is that it?"

"No. Another time I sold a puppy to the right people and bought it back and sold it to the wrong people, who got it stolen. The right people I *thought* the wrong people were kids in a garage band who wanted the dog to protect their equipment. When I got there to buy back the puppy, it was on the knee of one of the boys, watching cartoons with them. *I took the dog back*. Then I resold it to a family man who had children not yet rock 'n' roll age. He managed to let the dog be stolen, which the rock 'n' roll boys would never have done. And what would protect the boys' amps and drums and guitars now? My point is that my entire life is probably just a series of this kind of blind self-serving fuckup. *Everything* is cardinal-nest robbing and taking puppies from watching cartoons with their devoted new masters. *Every breath is dumb*. Even if you are on to this, you have no way of proving it. But the principle of reasonable doubt obtains. There is reasonable doubt that I have done one sensible thing in my life."

"Is that it?"

"That's it."

"You need to chill."

"To what?"

"Chill."

"Are you black?"

"Do I look black?"

"My point is, let them have their baby cardinals. Don't put them on your paddle," Mr. Albemarle said.

"Oh, brother."

"Are we having a fight?"

"No, babe. We are going to bed. You're a case."

"Well, bully for me."

Dale Mae smelled of gun oil, and Mr. Albemarle kissed her recoil shoulder, imagining it slightly empurpled from her shooting, but it was not. Her shoulder was pale and strong. She cleared his head of broken saws and wheeling gulls and writhing blue baby birds and misplaced dogs.

He put all of what was left of his desire, dumb or twisted or not, on top of and in this Dale Mae, and went through the motions, which is to say, vulgarly, made *the* motion, the curious in-out yes-no which all primates figure out or they die out, and it was a more or less standard bed-roll except that not only did Mr. Albemarle's astral body levitate above them but *two* astral bodies levitated above them, and impersonally looked at him doing this personal thing. This always happened with his one astral body, but with these his two astral bodies the impersonal viewing of his doing the personal thing, yessing noing yessing, was in stereo, as if he were a card in the trombone slide of a stereopticon.

As happens in that moment when the illusion of three dimensions obtains, Mr. Albemarle felt himself deepening, receding, *going in*. He lost himself in the picture a bit, or altogether, and lost himself in the personal thing, in the vulgar, in the sublime, in Dale Mae, in a hallowed and haunted way that 3-D pictures viewed this way can be hallowed and haunted, more rich-seeming than the flat life that their two separate views depict. He left his common dimensions. He got into it.

His mind decamped. He thought he saw the sodiers for a moment on his left, the aliens to his right, in tiered banks and waving at him as if he were on a float in a parade. He looked at Dale Mae but did not see her clearly — more precisely, he saw clearly *into her pores* if he saw clearly anything at all. The watchtower *was* getting softer, he thought, absurdly. The brick was turning to mush, his mind was turning to mush, he did not much mind. Had he been in the tiers of parade watchers waving, he would happily have waved at himself going by, or rather down, the street, or the tunnel, down whatever, wherever he was going, happily, down. He had waited a long time for once-was-lost-now-am-found, and he had no reservations about its general oddness or peculiar particulars. Dale Mae herself was already behind him, a warm soft old way of being. He was a new man, even if that meant, as it seemed to, not being exactly a man. That — exactness — was exactly what was being lost. It was being lost with an inexact agreeableness that felt at once intellectually irresponsible and shrewd. Mr. Albemarle was gone.

My Dinner with Jasper Johns (and Robert Rauschenberg, Leo Castelli, Robert and Ethel Scull, Willem de Kooning, Franz Kline and Lots More)

From the Journals of
Richard Brown Baker

Dramatis Personae

RICHARD BROWN BAKER: A collector of contemporary art, a Yale graduate and former Rhodes Scholar, he has the patrician bearing one would expect of the only son in a prominent Rhode Island family whose forebears arrived on the Mayflower. His ability to spot new talent has made him one of the foremost collectors of our time. In 1995 he donated his entire collection, valued at over $24.5 million, to Yale. He has been keeping a journal since the age of seven.

LEO CASTELLI: A gallery owner since 1957, he launched Rauschenberg and Johns with their first one-man shows in 1958.

ANTOINETTE: Castelli's partner for the evening, "Toiny" is an intelligent, worldly, slim blond with boycut bangs. Castelli later divorced his wife and married her.

DOROTHY MILLER: Curator of the museum collections at the Museum of Modern Art. Her ailing husband, HOLGER CAHILL, directed the Works Progress Administration projects under Roosevelt, was an early champion of modernism and a promoter of native American art.

JASPER JOHNS: His solo show at Castelli in 1958 made him "the darling of the art world's bright, brittle avant-garde." On the occasion of the Scull dinner, it is his thirtieth birthday.

ROBERT RAUSCHENBERG: His first show at Castelli in 1958 also made art history with his "madly inventive combines — half painting, half sculpture." With Johns, then his close friend, he is considered a cofounder of the pop-art school.

MARGARET BARR: An art historian and teacher at the Spence School, she is the wife and assistant to Alfred Barr, Jr., MOMA's founding director.

ROBERT (BOB) and ETHEL SCULL: The host and hostess. The Sculls are on their way to becoming the world's most avid collectors of pop art, and both enjoy nothing more than entertaining art luminaries at evenings such as this one. A self-made businessman, Bob is often ridiculed for his lack of social skills and for his nouveaux riches, but admired for his good eye and collection.

MRS. HARRIS: A guest of the Sculls.

MY DINNER WITH JASPER JOHNS

SIDNEY JANIS and HARRIET (HANSI) JANIS: Gallery owners since 1948, they represent Willem de Kooning, Franz Kline, Jackson Pollock and other major abstract expressionists.
FRANZ KLINE: The action painter famous for his black and white calligraphic paintings. He died in 1962.
BETSY ZOGBAUM: Kline's girlfriend after the death of her husband, Wilfred "Zog" Zogbaum, a sculptor. Formerly a neighbor and friend of Jackson Pollock and Lee Krasner.
WILLEM DE KOONING: The Dutch-born abstract expressionist.
RUTH KLIGMAN: An aspiring painter who was Pollock's last lover.
DAVID SOLINGER: An art collector and chairman of the board of trustees at the Whitney Museum. His wife, HOPE GIMBEL SOLINGER, is from the famed department-store family.

—Johanna Garfield

•

May 15, 1960

I have shamefully neglected this diary, in which I had meant to chronicle the art life of our metropolis, but the botheration of Christmas was too much for me. I dammed up, and until this sunny May morning, have had not the tiniest inclination to write a word in it.

But I think I should capture a reference to last night's dinner party. I'm unlikely to attend many such. Besides, in a couple of weeks the art season in New York will have ended. Dealers, museum people, artists, all will shortly be off to Europe . . .

Our host and hostess were Mr. and Mrs. Robert Scull of Blue Sea Lane, Great Neck, Long Island. The Sculls began scarcely four years ago to collect contemporary art. He is wealthy, it is said, through the ownership of a fleet of several hundred taxicabs. Well, it isn't especially relevant how he came by his money. The interesting thing is how he is spending it, and boy, has he spent a fortune on the new art of today! No, perhaps I shouldn't say that, because even his oils and drawings by de Kooning, his enormous Kline, his paintings by Jasper Johns and collages by Robert Rauschenberg, his sculptures by John Chamberlain and others, although they have required the outlay of countless thousands, have not in totality approached the prices millionaires pay for Renoirs, Seurats and Gauguins. At least by my piker's standards!

The Sculls are still a young couple with three small sons, one of whom, Johnny, is quite an active artist. Bob Scull himself paints. Interspersed among the modern treasures on the wide high walls of this low-lying, spreading, contemporary house (from whose big windows one gets a view of Great Neck Bay) are pictures created by both father and son. They don't look incongruous, either.

Mr. Scull sent his Cadillac into Manhattan with his personal chauffeur to pick up a group of us at the Leo Castelli Gallery. I came there at 6:30. Leo's wife is ill and hospitalized. An attractive young Frenchwoman was on hand as Leo's partner for the evening. The vivacious Dorothy Miller of the Museum of Modern Art and her aged husband, Holger Cahill, came next. Finally, rather late, arrived Leo's two most phenomenally successful young artists: Jasper Johns (whose thirtieth birthday we observed with a cake when it began at midnight) and Robert Rauschenberg.

Bob Rauschenberg's sleek white Jaguar was waiting downstairs, and when we set out, Dorothy Miller went with this young pair, whose work she included in her recent, much denounced exhibit, "Sixteen Americans." (Virginia Field — or was it Dorothy Miller? — once startled me by asking of Johns and Rauschenberg, "They shack up, don't they?")

The front seat of the Cadillac was shared by the colored chauffeur with Leo and his girlfriend, while I sat in back with Holger Cahill and Margaret Barr, whom we picked up at the corner of Ninety-sixth Street near her home. Her husband, Alfred Jr., whom I'm sure the Sculls were very anxious to have see their collection, had gone bird-watching to the country for the weekend and was thus absent from an occasion that I doubt not was planned partly in his honor, although this was actually a postponement of about six weeks from the first planned date, which was made impossible by the death of Bob Scull's father.

Robert Rauschenberg, Interior 2, *1958.*

As we drove to Great Neck—the trip requires about forty-five minutes—Margaret Barr and Leo Castelli talked about their plan for their summer visits to Europe: towns in Italy, flight expenses, hotels preferred. All the while, the Jaguar was following us closely.

We arrived scarcely five minutes late and as we stepped from our cars, were at once fascinated by the garden with its flowers and sculpture that nestled between the house and the slope of the hill on whose bank the house was situated. The hillside had been cut away and shored up with rough-cut beams of wood.

Then out came Bob Scull to greet us, followed by Ethel, superbly gowned in a dramatic black dress by Dior. Her houseguest, Mrs. Harris, a Frenchwoman who married an Englishman, was equally smartly gowned in white satin. Both looked like Parisian models in their chicness. Mrs. Harris was bejeweled in dazzling fashion. We were brought inside, past a small oil by de Kooning that is one of the few of his paintings I have instantly liked, into the long, open drawing room. One side of it, which faces the view of the bay, is all windows. At the far end, over the fireplace, hangs a vivid-hued abstraction by Franz Kline that must be a dozen or fifteen feet long.

Margaret Barr and I had the same idea, however. Before dusk passed into dark, we wanted to see the garden. Art could wait. We were outdoors on the paved terrace when the remaining guests arrived, Sidney Janis and his Hansi, Franz Kline and his girlfriend, Betsy Zogbaum, and Willem de Kooning with his girlfriend, Ruth Kligman. She is the young woman who, as I understand it, once enjoyed the affections of Jackson Pollock and was in the car with him at the time of his fatal accident. I was curious to see this woman who seems to have belonged to two of our leading artists. She was wearing a black, low-neck dress, tight around the waist and with a short flaring skirt. Although it was more formal than the severe gray suit (not evening wear at all) in which Betsey Zogbaum was dressed, it looked rather tawdry to me compared to Ethel Scull's beautiful gown.

Another pair of guests was David and Hope Solinger. David Solinger at one time was a good client of Sam Kootz [*a famous*

MY DINNER WITH JASPER JOHNS

art dealer at the time], and served as his lawyer, but last weekend, while staying at the Kootzes in the country, I learned that they have had a falling out. Sam referred to David as "one of the worst chiselers" in the art field. Anyway, David Solinger is a collector of contemporary art, and quite a few years ago gave the Museum of Modern Art a black and white painting by Franz Kline. This season, he bought another Kline. I remember him telling me also of his purchase of a small oil by Bill de Kooning when de Kooning was totally unestablished. For the painting, he paid only a couple of hundred dollars. De Kooning was so broke that he asked for five dollars of the amount in cash.

Willem de Kooning, Collage and Crayon, *1960.*

Since then, the pendulum has swung indeed. Rumors say that both de Kooning and Kline earn over $100,000 a year.

I was indeed dining with the new rich of the art world. I was surprised when Margaret Barr asked to be introduced to Mr. Kline. How could she not have met him sooner?

We went back into the house. At one side of the living room was a built-in bar. Cocktails were being served. I asked for vodka and, there being none, took a dry martini in substitute. For some while before settling down to conversation, I wandered about looking at the Sculls' art. I admired their choices.

Negro menservants and a maid constantly passed among us offering a greater quantity and variety of hors d'oeuvres than I have seen anywhere this season except at a plush cocktail party given in the Four Seasons Restaurant by Phyllis Lambert in honor of a French painter named François Arnal. At that function, the edibles were beyond all my experience. Yet the Sculls weren't far behind. The trays contained so much that was tempting that before we were called to dinner, I ate nearly a meal of snacks. Later, Betsy Zogbaum confided to me that she had been unable to eat any of the dinner proper because before setting out, being hungry, she had asked Franz to get her a bite, and once arrived, she had thought the hors d'oeuvres constituted the dinner. This error was understandable because, parallel to the room we occupied during cocktails, could be seen the regular dining room. The Scull dinner table was not set for sit-down guests but instead was covered with plates of hors d'oeuvres as if it were a buffet.

At 9:30, nearly two hours after our arrival, we were taken downstairs to be seated in a huge basement room at three tables. This room contained the best painting by Al Leslie I've ever seen, a small Nassos Daphnis, a large Raymond Parker (on approval, Bob Scull told me) and a magnificent sculpture by John Chamberlain. At my table the host himself presided, with Dorothy Miller on his right and Margaret Barr on his left. I sat between Leo Castelli's French girlfriend and Jasper Johns, whose nickname I learned from his place card is Jaap.

I was reminded of a panel discussion at New York University

Jasper Johns, The Small Figure 3, *1960.*

about contemporary art I'd attended a few weeks ago at which several artists from the "Sixteen Americans" show, including Johns and Rauschenberg, were participants. Louise Nevelson and Richard Stankiewicz were others on the panel. The evening promised well, and I persuaded the young English painter

Richard Smith to attend with me. But oh, what an aimless, dismal, boring discussion it turned out to be! Robert Goldwater, the moderator, gave no guidance. Many in the audience left. Individual speakers were at moments excellent, but the evening as a whole was a failure.

I talked of this occasion with Jasper Johns, who defended young Frank Stella from the criticism I made of his role, and who spoke with asperity of Richard Stankiewicz (who at one point shouted "Nonsense!" to a remark of Stella's). I personally was more impressed by Stankiewicz's statements than by any others of the evening, but I did not tell Johns that, as I could see that he dislikes Richard. He said he himself had not wanted to participate, agreed that the occasion turned out badly and yet would be willing to attempt another such discussion.

Alas, I could not find much to talk about with the French girl.

We were served a dinner of many courses, the principal dish being Rock Cornish guinea hen. We had side dishes of salad and drank champagne. The most unexpected feature of the feast came toward the end. The waiter passed a platter of strawberries with a center bowl of whipped cream. Everyone took some of this dessert. But it was barely on our plates when another waiter appeared with a chocolate roll with chocolate sauce. My neighbors turned this down, but I am greedy and helped myself. No sooner was this chocolate mass nestled upon the plate beside the strawberries than a third waiter stood by me offering an apricot cream pudding. This I naturally declined, but Jaap took some. I thought to myself of Trimalchio's famous banquet and suspected this might be my closest analogous experience.

Coffee was served to us at table. By this time we had been long seated. Mrs. Barr looked across the table at Jasper Johns and remarked, "Let's you and I exchange seats. We've been sitting a long time in these."

"Why should I?" asked Johns. He made no motion to rise. Her proposal was inexplicable to him. It was then arranged that Mrs. Barr and Dorothy Miller should exchange places, which meant merely that they shifted from one side of their host to another.

Later, when we had risen and gone upstairs, I sat for a time on a sofa with Betsy Zogbaum and Hope Gimbel Solinger. Brandy was offered, which I declined. Before long I became thirsty, however. I went to the bar behind which Bob Scull was standing and asked for iced soda flavored with whiskey. Ruth Kligman was also at the bar. She looked—stared—at me and said, "I don't know who you are."

Bob Scull said, "This is Richard Brown Baker,"

"I have never heard of you," she answered. Ruth's eyes are lustrous and dark. They are the striking feature in a somewhat coarsely voluptuous face.

I said lamely, "There is no particular reason for anyone to hear of me," and thought to myself, This woman exists for the bed.

Getting my beverage, I went to talk with Mrs. Barr and someone else. Eventually, Ruth approached Mrs. Barr and said, "I like you better this evening than I did the last time we met."

With cold equanimity, Mrs. Barr replied, "I am not accustomed to being liked."

Ruth went on, "You were very, very angry then."

As a diarist, I am sorry that I heard no more of this exchange. It virtually came to an end there, Ruth yielding the field and withdrawing.

Mrs. Barr talked about Picasso and his "Midas touch" with such asperity that I observed, "You have little affection for him."

"I have affection for few people," she replied. "I choose them carefully. Yes, I have no affection for Picasso." She then told of a luncheon on the Riviera when she and Alfred were with Picasso at his habitual restaurant in town. In strode the movie star Gary Cooper, and Picasso was tremendously pleased to see him. He told the actor to draw something for him. Gary Cooper made a small sketch of a cowboy. Picasso was delighted. It came Picasso's turn to do a quick drawing. Mrs.

Barr said he did it with his nail on a table cloth. "And this is what I mean by the Midas touch. Everything he draws turns to gold so he did it in a way that guaranteed it wouldn't last." Picasso is not a generous man, she contends.

Franz Kline, Untitled, *1951.*

I noticed Franz Kline come and sit beside Bob Rauschenberg. It looked to me as if Kline had imbibed too much to talk naturally. I felt no desire to talk to Kline or to de Kooning myself. I wonder why. Perhaps as an aspiring painter, I am jealous of their eminence.

I saw Ruth Kligman and Bill de Kooning stand together. She kissed him amorously on the lips and he kissed the curve of her neck. Later, I saw Ruth kissing Sidney Janis, and still later she was embracing Leo Castelli. I also noticed that Dorothy Miller took her elderly husband downstairs, probably to afford him an opportunity to rest. Or maybe she was afraid Ruth would pick him as the next object of her affection.

An unexpected gesture of hospitality was the appearance (about half an hour after the midnight serving of Jaap's birthday cake) of a platter artistically arranged with cool slices of fresh pineapple and melon. When it came time to return to New York, it became evident that Dorothy Miller planned to sit in the Cadillac with her husband. As this would have put four of us in the back seat, I suggested that there might be less discomfort if I became a passenger in the Jaguar. I didn't realize that Jasper Johns would have to squeeze into a narrow rear area as a result, but he did, and I had the fun of returning to town with these two young artists, whom I find agreeable and different.

They spoke as if it had been a testy evening on many scores. I had heard Bob Rauschenberg have a taut exchange with our hostess. Ethel chided him for not having personally accepted for the dinner. She said she had had to find out that he was coming through Leo and Jaap. He took this rebuke in a kidding way, which led to an exchange approaching the character of a quarrel.

From the rear, Jasper Johns asked, "Who is this fellow Solinger?" He had evidently had a bitter dispute with him. I think he was a trifle disconcerted when I answered that Solinger is a lawyer, amateur painter, well-known collector and active in leadership of the Whitney Museum.

I have often wondered what Mr. Scull, who was nice enough to have us all to dinner, made of the bickering that went on.

Pattiann Rogers

The Composer, the Bone Yard

Across my work yard the bones lie,
a rubble in crests and waves, piled
white, grooved brown, ocean to ocean—
dirt, ash, bevel, hovel. The rib staves
hold their swell like breath held. Fetal
cartilages curl, dead in their dead
pelvis bowls, hard seeds stopped
in fossil blossoms, pearl stones
in cracked shells.

I dig and scrape, horizon
to horizon, unearth, unheaven,
fasten and hinge great saber tusks
and broken mandibles, tiny notches
smaller than dormouse fang,
titmouse toe. I latch and lock
together the fractured pieces—ball,
joint, hammer—sew and seam
with brass threads, fit pegs
into their corresponding jigsaw
hooks, count my knotted strings
and bands. I untangle, match,
mend, lathe the past-to-come
in this graveyard where I work.

Sometimes I think I feel the splintered
herds beginning to emerge whole
and in motion, the fallen flocks
to sound and wing. Perhaps I see

dry fish skeletons come weaving
out of rock to water. Resurrection
is my work and belief my resurrection.

The composing pattern of these bones
is the only world I possess, the eye
of my eye, the measure of my ear,
the defined day of the definition to be
when finally fully assembled I can rise,
shaking off dust and rain, roaring,
many-voiced, many-bodied, and raucous
with new hungers.

Two Poems by Alan Michael Parker

Orpheus in New England

Something about the ironing board made him
leave it behind, angular in the emptied living room,

beautiful as a heron, all nobility
a form of use. It could stand for years.
It could fill its skin as only an object can.

Something about that final 5 A.M.,
not wanting to look back, unwilling to stop

as the future idled in the drive, leaning on a horn.
He knew he was too old for all this regret—
not a heron but a fossil; no, not a fossil

but a letter of some kind—too old
for all he had been, in the tomb of his being.

Gray coffee plashes in a travel cup, the morning
fog a second mortgage on last night.
And with each perfect house he passed

he could almost see the heron unfold
its complicated bones, blink one stormy eye

and ready itself for flight: to circle the ceiling,
arc over the coat tree, then fill the upstairs
with wingbeats and the blur of immanence.

Aubade: The Hotel Cleveland

Through the drapes the moon lounges like Achilles.
Sprawled on the bed the moon lounges like Achilles.

I can hear you in the bathroom: rinsing, splashing, steaming;
Three different kinds of sound slurred, the elements
Confounded by your actions. (Across the airshaft,

The all-night revelers have finally pulled their revels closed.
Quiet comes to spy, to lurk in a drunken dream.)

Where I was, where you were, the air set
Around us, love. Set and settled. Formed.
Through the drapes the moon lounges like Achilles.

At the edge, in a tent along the Flats, the sun.
An elevator rises, announces, hushes, descends.

Sprawled on the bed the moon lounges like Achilles.
(The part of us necessarily alone has come to stay.)
I can hear water trickling to a conclusion,

Habitual, carrying on, suspended in itself.
What will be: you open the bathroom door and then . . .

I sit up in bed to the sound of traffic,
A muscle car convulsing in an alley.
Through the drapes, washed away,

The moon lolls, leans against its shield.
An elevator rises, announces, hushes, descends.

Rika Lesser

536 Saratoga Avenue

Driving by it now—walking in Brownsville
is no longer safe—536 remains
the only semi-private house on the block.
Everything else has changed: The tenements
across the street are gone. Nothing
replaces them. On our side, burnt and
blown-out frames surround empty courtyards.

Long before I was born, my mother's family
bought the house. Grandmother Ruchtcha died.
I bear the English name she took at
Immigration. Had she not died, I would be
someone else—a name is powerful.

Sharing a bedroom with my middle sister,
I wondered why the playroom was not my own.
Too young to remember Grandfather's moving
out. He lived nearby, across a busy street,
then in the downstairs flat, then in a "home."
Finally, he lived with us; the playroom his again.

My eldest sister had the long front room.
In the street you knew when she talked
on the telephone: she'd stick her feet
out the jalousie windows. Now a wide
strip of tape masks a bifurcation.

Of course, there were other rooms, other doors,
but one of those farthest back completes the tour.

The full bath was called "Rika's bathroom"
because I hogged it. In my sleep I'd walk there.
Awake I'd drown my toys, imagining the room
to be an island. Shipwrecked, I allowed myself
a large box of cream-filled cookies. With water,
soft towels, the clothing in the hamper,
I'd do all right. I won't allow myself to imagine
what goes on there now. What the small black boy,
who rode a tricycle when we drove past
last summer, would think if he found
scratched with the head of a safety-pin
on the tile wall beneath the towel rod
my name.

Two Poems by Lance Larsen

Nest

The things I saved up there—mantis legs, cat fur,
porcupine quills tied with twine. I thought
this was religion. To climb through leaves

and pocked apples to the highest bough, to finger
what no one else wanted. Cicada husk,
dried fish tail. Not death, but what it left

behind. I touched tongue to rabbit skull, tasted
the eye holes. So many creeds, and only a crooked
wind and the sulfur glow of the railroad yards

to help do the sorting. Snake skin wrapping
my knuckles, the clink of wisdom teeth, my aunt's.
Worn down enough to make me think of food.

What it might mean to chew. And be chewed.
That divination. Then putting everything
back. Bone puzzle, flesh pieced against fur.

And swallowing as I climbed down—the creature
above and inside me now. Anything left over
circling like an owl or accidental prayer.

Interview

A problem *muy adentro*, she tells him, deep
inside her—a metal loop like a piece
of Satan, but the doctor who was supposed
to remove it on vacation. All the while
her hands churning at her belt line
like paddle wheels. To this, add crying.
And now her question: Can God make her
clean with this coiled thing still inside?

This the baptismal interview, this
the gringo elder's first confession
from a girl his age. Between them,
a dirtied scratch on the kitchen table.
A paring knife and sliced pomegranate.
Is it him, or the room? Some sort of pulsing.
He does not want to picture the loop.
Or watch the hands churning. He wants
to build a church for her out of his words,
invite her to pass inside. Instead,
wounds splay the walls, her closed-eyed
lovers squirming the table. He keeps
his eyes moving. When he speaks—his voice,
but inside him a burning like a flock
of birds. *Renewal, font, Jesus—*
words that hover, then pass between them.
They seem inside out and too small.

He opens his book to a clean page. Writes
name and birth date. Then her city,
which he keeps spelling wrong. *La Cisterna*,
she says. Cistern. Like this—a vessel,
a place of water. The room gathers
at her fingers and she makes a pitcher
out of air. Holds before him what nestles
inside her. He has crossed some barrier,

he knows, this boy who in nineteen years
has been with no one but himself. He
is saying what sounds like God's name.
Asking for something. Darkness maybe.
Or blood. He knows it has to do with thirst.

Claire Bateman

Ectoplasm

For the base I prefer a paste of unscented soap, egg white, &
    glue or gelatin, often peroxide—
never, as do some of my competitors, chewed muslin strips
    or (loathsome!) bits of animal tissue!
Though receiving but five dollars each night at the lyceum
    (a dollar at home),
I am an artist!
I can cause the luminous webbing to stream out from my
    fingertips,
plastic though not wholly passive, diaphanous but of a
    palpable density,
slightly sticky while also ductile & fluent,
shimmering as it forms the most novel of apports—a harp,
strings plucked by a little breeze from nowhere,
a bouquet of translucent tulips, exquisitely formed . . .
I have conjured the hovering images of Mr. Douglas & the
    honorably scraggy Mr. Lincoln—
though both of them yet live!—
as if plucking their etheric bodies from the place where each
    dwells locked within the other's opposition.
And I can produce for any patron the ghost of her stillborn,
can make it speak, voice emanating from the floating spirit
    horn
or directly from the tiny radiant corpus:
Where I abide, mother, there is no chill, no ache.
Together my brothers & I,
we wait for you!

But to those of the True Gift,
the spirit world is nothing if not generous;

from the age of thirteen to thirty-three,
I had only to light the candle, close my eyes, attune my
   thoughts, & I would begin to tremble as with a palsy
as a swift sequence of electric thrills ran up my spine
& I smelled the sharp scent of the air just after a rain
while from my mouth, ears, nostrils, & tear ducts
poured a vapor that swirled about me, clinging, then
   thickening
to a waterfall of slim threads
like a bridal veil, a spider web,
or the rigging of a ship sailing so swiftly it seems becalmed.
Gauzy yet copious: a shocking profusion!
I have heard speculation that it comes from the spaces between
   the cells of one's earthly flesh—
the kingdom of heaven is within us?
Old news!
For those two decades I nightly communed in this way,
beheld the emanations take on shapes as they willed—
a tiara that burned with cold flame, crowning me,
a bodiless winged head singing to me in French,
even an infant with trailing placenta—
I nursed this babe with my phosphorescent milk, overflowing,
most certainly, a virgin birth!

Why then did I cease these transmissions,
divert my energies to mere artifice?
Because ecstasy is tiresome.
It plays with us & plays us,
for the spirit realm has nothing better to do!
My soul became parched & shrunken,
like those hideous heads that savages have scooped out &
   boiled down!
Strolling in the afternoons through market or park,
I *saw* all—the secrets behind each face, their places in the
   Great Plan—
but I *felt* nothing,
nothing human.
Yes, wherever you find glory, spiritual exaltation,

look also for a certain numbness, vacuity,
a victim!
There is always a victim,
often willing,
frequently, more than one.
For not only through the sisterhood of the elect
do They seek to break through, break through.
Think of the inebriation of battle,
the blissful rage of Beethoven's Ninth.
Beware the surge from the deep,
the wave cresting, triumphant—
there will be corpses, I tell you,
bodies broken & strewn—

And afterward,
from the Other Side,
fatigue, bewilderment,
as that of a child exhausted from some unchecked willful
    frenzy.
O to give comfort then!
To open oneself for Them to slake Their thirst!
But one must be pitiless.
One must then & ever
attempt to extricate oneself,
to replace mystic consummation
with craft, simulation,
the textures of the terrestrial plane,
that the soul may come to find some degree of relief—
I do not say cure!—
from its devotion to glory,
if such recovery be possible.

Disclaimer

David Means

Disclaimer: Nothing in this story is true. All of the characters in this story are products of the writer's imagination. Any likeness of these characters and the situation described herein to those in real life are purely coincidental. In the unlikely circumstance that one or more of the characters in this story bear any resemblance to those living or dead, please be forewarned that it is so out of random chance (any other kind being excluded). Although the events in this story were drawn from real circumstances, this is in all ways a work of the imagination. Perhaps there might be characters like Julie Row in real life; if so, the author would like to express, if necessary before a court of law, that this work came to fruition in his imagination and all said resemblances to her are matters of chance. In the unlikelihood that there is a young woman living in the Stonewood Condominiums, who rolls her hair up in the old plastic kind of curlers—prickly pink rolls with pink clamp shells—and wears a fine hair net over them while she sleeps, if there is someone matching that description, the author would like to deny any a priori knowledge of the fact; even if said Julie Row lived by herself, had a tabby named

Marvin, and was on the night of July 15, 1991, the night of her murder, alone and sad and feeling the soft night breeze work through the screen; even if said Julie Row had once been with a guy named Rudy, and that Rudy had applied the hot, orange butt of his cigarette to the back of her wrist in a flaming moment (of panic and desire) — his version of some kind of religious sacrament — the author will bear no responsibility for similarities therein: thus if the said Julie Row, lying back on the couch, her flat white stomach exposed, the knot of her belly button — (an "outie") — picks the phone up to call her mother, Mrs. Joanna Row of 415 Park Street, and says, "Mom it's Julie how you doing?" only to hear her mother's sharp middle-western voice say, "Do I know someone by such a name?" and therefore flatly denying any human connection with her daughter, who just stares long into the phone receiver, holding it back, and then off at the blue flick of the television screen, and then outside at the flat asphalt parking lot where others such as her while away the last of a hot summer day — should, through some pure coincidences, this conversation exist in real life, the author would once again state: THIS WORK IS THE PRODUCT OF THE AUTHOR'S IMAGINATION, even if Mrs. Joanna Row lay down on her own divan after her phone was back in the cradle, her long, narrow face tight with a bitterness certain readers in Alma, Michigan might recognize, and cried tears (of remorse and anger), such tears being similar to said person — in that case the author would, if necessary, bring to court expert testimony as to the preponderance of such tears in small towns (all over America). And if on July 15, 1991, said Julie Row after listening to her mother's words, having turned to the television and then back to those outside, spotted a guy named Bub leaning against his jacked-up Toyota four-wheeler with the boom box going, who had a thing for watching Julie in her white halter top when she hung by the pool, and who once, while Rudy (her current main squeeze) was diving beneath the glistening aqua-blue water, copped a quick feel from Julie, who turned, blushed, and in the process became aware one might assume of certain moral certitudes broken in the course of hanging around with a guy like Rudy, around men like Bub — after said character has looked out the window, stands, responding to a soft knock on the door, and straightens the edges of her powder-blue terry shorts and pulls back on the hollow-centered door to reveal Bub himself; and should said character Bub, six-five, heavyweight, self-inflicted tattoos on his knuckles spelling BUB, with a small Fu Manchu — should said character actually exist in Alma, Michigan, with legal records corresponding to a man by that name tallying up several counts of aggravated assault, petty larceny, burglary, should someone by that name exist, and with said characteristics, the author would like to state, emphatically, that this unlikely resemblance between the product of his imagination and the world at large is PURELY AN ACT OF COINCIDENCE; and should it be brought to the court's attention that on the said night of July 15, 1991, a man with the description above was seen standing at the door of apartment 12 of the Stonewood complex, while the sprinkler system went on, spraying skyward a vast mist spanning all four units of the complex facing westward, drawing from the asphalt and the grass a musty odor, dank and rich, consuming those hanging around their cars, including Bub, with a sudden, short-lived memory flash of bygone summer days when the combination of dry earth and sudden rain brought out a dreamy primal memory of days when kids ran through barley fields, broke back cornstalks, and lay at times for no good reason facedown on sweet grass and listened to the earth move — a time when rain and dry earth shattered each other; days, this memory flash held, when there was an innocence to be spoken of — should said Bub have stood at the door under these conditions, the author would, again, like it to be clearly known that this work is purely a product of his imagination; although certain details have been drawn from REAL LIFE, ANY RESEMBLANCE TO PERSONS LIVING OR DEAD OR OTHERWISE IS PURELY COINCIDENTAL. AMEN.

Marvin, and was on the night of July 15, 1991, the night of her murder, alone and sad and feeling the soft night breeze work through the screen; even if said Julie Row had once been with a guy named Rudy, and that Rudy had applied the hot, orange butt of his cigarette to the back of her wrist in a flaming moment (of panic and desire) — his version of some kind of religious sacrament — the author will bear no responsibility for similarities therein: thus if the said Julie Row, lying back on the couch, her flat white stomach exposed, the knot of her belly button — (an "outie") — picks the phone up to call her mother, Mrs. Joanna Row of 415 Park Street, and says, "Mom it's Julie how you doing?" only to hear her mother's sharp middle-western voice say, "Do I know someone by such a name?" and therefore flatly denying any human connection with her daughter, who just stares long into the phone receiver, holding it back, and then off at the blue flick of the television screen, and then outside at the flat asphalt parking lot where others such as her while away the last of a hot summer day — should, through some pure coincidences, this conversation exist in real life, the author would once again state: THIS WORK IS THE PRODUCT OF THE AUTHOR'S IMAGINATION, even if Mrs. Joanna Row lay down on her own divan after her phone was back in the cradle, her long, narrow face tight with a bitterness certain readers in Alma, Michigan might recognize, and cried tears (of remorse and anger), such tears being similar to said person — in that case the author would, if necessary, bring to court expert testimony as to the preponderance of such tears in small towns (all over America). And if on July 15, 1991, said Julie Row after listening to her mother's words, having turned to the television and then back to those outside, spotted a guy named Bub leaning against his jacked-up Toyota four-wheeler with the boom box going, who had a thing for watching Julie in her white halter top when she hung by the pool, and who once, while Rudy (her current main squeeze) was diving beneath the glistening aqua-blue water, copped a quick feel from Julie, who turned, blushed, and in the process became aware one might assume of certain moral certitudes broken in the course of hanging around with a guy like Rudy, around men like Bub—after said character has looked out the window, stands, responding to a soft knock on the door, and straightens the edges of her powder-blue terry shorts and pulls back on the hollow-centered door to reveal Bub himself; and should said character Bub, six-five, heavyweight, self-inflicted tattoos on his knuckles spelling BUB, with a small Fu Manchu—should said character actually exist in Alma, Michigan, with legal records corresponding to a man by that name tallying up several counts of aggravated assault, petty larceny, burglary, should someone by that name exist, and with said characteristics, the author would like to state, emphatically, that this unlikely resemblance between the product of his imagination and the world at large is PURELY AN ACT OF COINCIDENCE; and should it be brought to the court's attention that on the said night of July 15, 1991, a man with the description above was seen standing at the door of apartment 12 of the Stonewood complex, while the sprinkler system went on, spraying skyward a vast mist spanning all four units of the complex facing westward, drawing from the asphalt and the grass a musty odor, dank and rich, consuming those hanging around their cars, including Bub, with a sudden, short-lived memory flash of bygone summer days when the combination of dry earth and sudden rain brought out a dreamy primal memory of days when kids ran through barley fields, broke back cornstalks, and lay at times for no good reason facedown on sweet grass and listened to the earth move—a time when rain and dry earth shattered each other; days, this memory flash held, when there was an innocence to be spoken of— should said Bub have stood at the door under these conditions, the author would, again, like it to be clearly known that this work is purely a product of his imagination; although certain details have been drawn from REAL LIFE, ANY RESEMBLANCE TO PERSONS LIVING OR DEAD OR OTHERWISE IS PURELY COINCIDENTAL. AMEN.

NOTES ON CONTRIBUTORS

FICTION

David Means is the author of *A Quick Kiss of Redemption*, a collection of short stories. He is at work on a novel and lives in Nyack, New York.

Joyce Carol Oates is the author most recently of the novel *We Were the Mulvaneys* and the novella *First Love*. She was the 1996 recipient of the PEN/Malamud Award for Achievement in the Short Story. She lives and teaches in Princeton, New Jersey.

Padgett Powell is the author of five books of fiction, including the short-story collection *Aliens of Affection*, which will be published by Henry Holt this winter. He teaches at the University of Florida.

Charlie Smith is the author of five books of fiction, including *Cheap Ticket to Heaven*, *Shine Hawk* (published by Paris Review Editions) and *Crystal River*, the title novella of which won this magazine's Aga Khan Prize for fiction. His fifth collection of poems, *Life on Earth*, will be published by W. W. Norton next year.

POETRY

Claire Bateman's first collection of poetry, *The Bicycle Slow Race*, was published in 1991, and her second, *Friction*, will appear at the end of the year. She received a NEA Literary Fellowship in 1991.

Bruce Bond is the director of creative writing at University of North Texas and poetry editor for the *American Literary Review*. His third collection of poetry, *Radiography*, is forthcoming.

Nicholas Christopher is the author of six books of poetry, most recently, *5°* and *X rays*, which is forthcoming. He has written two novels, *The Soloist* and *Veronica*, which was reprinted this year, and a study of film noir, *Somewhere in the Night: Film Noir and The American City*. He is at work on a new novel, *A Trip to the Stars*.

Brian Culhane's poetry has appeared most recently in *The New Republic*, *Boulevard* and *The Gettysburg Review*. He lives in Seattle where he teaches English at the Lakeside School.

Barbara Goldberg is the author of five books: *Berta Broadfoot and Pepin the Short: A Merovingian Romance*, *Cautionary Tales*, *This Terrible Thing Called Love*, *Dear Paolo: Writings from the Quatrrocento*, and *Marvelous Pursuits*. She has coedited two books with the Israeli poet Moshe Dor, *The Stones Remember* and *After the First Rain: Israeli Poems on War and Peace*. She lives in Chevy Chase, Maryland.

Barbara Henning is the author of *Smoking in the Twilight Bar*, *Love Makes Thinking Dark* and the forthcoming *In Between*.

Andrew Hudgins's most recent book of poems is *The Glass Hammer*, and he has a collection of essays forthcoming as part of the Poets on Poetry Series, *The Glass Anvil*.

Lance Larsen's poetry has appeared in *The Hudson Review*, *Boulevard*, *New Republic*, *Salmagundi*, *Poetry Wales*, *Shenandoah* and elsewhere. He teaches at Brigham Young University.

Rika Lesser is the author of three collections of poetry, *Etruscan Things*, *All We Need of Hell* and *Growing Back: Poems 1972-1992*, which is forthcoming. She is also translator of many Swedish-language poets, among them Claes Andersson, Gunnar Ekelöf and Göran Sonnevi. In 1996 she received the Poetry Translation Prize of the Swedish Academy.

Sarah Lindsay's first book of poems, *Primate Behavior*, will appear this fall. She works as a copy editor in Greensboro, North Carolina.

William Logan's new book of poems, *Vain Empires*, and a book of essays and reviews, *Reputations of the Tongue*, are forthcoming.

W.S. Merwin's latest book of poems is *The Vixen*. He lives in Hawaii.

Michelangelo di Lodovico Buonarrotti Simoni (1475–1564) was an Italian sculptor, painter, architect and poet. His translator, **John Frederick Nims's** most recent books of poetry are *The Six-Cornered Snowflake* and *Zany in Denim*. His translation of Euripides' *Suppliant Women* will appear this fall.

Alan Michael Parker is coeditor of *The Routledge Anthology of Cross-Gendered Verse*, North American editor for *Who's Who in Twentieth Century Poetry* and author of a collection of poetry, *Days Like Prose*. He teaches at Penn State Erie, The Behrend College.

Amanda Pecor has poems forthcoming in *Journal* and *American Poetry Review*. She is completing a Ph.D. at the University of Utah, and is originally from Georgia.

NOTES ON CONTRIBUTORS

Pattiann Rogers's seventh book, *Eating Bread & Honey*, will appear in the fall.
Charles H. Webb is a rock singer turned psychotherapist and professor of English. His collection, *Reading the Water*, was chosen by Edward Hirsch as winner of the 1997 Morse Poetry Prize.
Rachel Wetzsteon's first book of poems, *The Other Stars*, won the 1993 National Poetry Series. A second book of poems, *Home and Away*, will be published next year.

FEATURES

Johanna Garfield has written about artists, museums and art shows for numerous magazines. She is the author of *The Life of a Real Girl, A True Story* and *Cousins*.
Dotson Rader is the author of *Tennessee: Cry of the Heart*. He is one of the contributors to *Truman Capote*, an oral biography forthcoming this December.
James Salter is the author of *A Sport and a Pastime* (now in Modern Library), *Light Years*, *Solo Faces* and *Dusk and Other Stories*, which won the PEN/Faulkner Award in 1988. The piece in this issue is from his memoir, *Burning the Days*, which will be published this fall. He lives in Colorado and Long Island.

INTERVIEWS

Leo Lerman (Jan Morris interview), who died in 1994, was editorial advisor at Condé Nast Publications.
George Plimpton (John le Carré interview) is the editor of *The Paris Review*. He is the author of several books, including *The X Factor* and the upcoming *Truman Capote*.

ART

Lynn McCarty is represented by the Nancy Hoffman Gallery in New York City.
Graham Nickson's large-scale drawings appear courtesy of Salander-O'Reilly Gallery.
Billy Sullivan's drawing appears courtesy of Fischbach Gallery.

The Paris Review Booksellers Advisory Board

THE PARIS REVIEW BOOKSELLERS ADVISORY BOARD is a group of owners and managers of independent bookstores from around the world who have agreed to share with us their knowledge and expertise.

ANDREAS BROWN, *Gotham Bookmart, New York, NY*
CHAPMAN, DRESCHER & PETERSON,
 Bloomsbury Bookstore, Ashland, OR
ROBERT CONTANT, *St. Mark's Bookstore, New York, NY*
JOHN EKLUND, *Harry W. Schwartz Bookshop, Milwaukee, WI*
JOSEPH GABLE, *Borders Bookshop, Ann Arbor, MI*
THOMAS GLADYSZ, *The Booksmith, San Francisco, CA*
HELENE GOLAY, *The Corner Bookstore, New York, NY*
GLEN GOLDMAN, *Booksoup, West Hollywood, CA*
JAMES HARRIS, *Prairie Lights Bookstore, Iowa City, IA*
ODILE HELLIER, *Village Voice, Paris, France*
RICHARD HOWORTH, *Square Books, Oxford, MS*
KARL KILIAN, *Brazos Bookstore, Houston, TX*
KRIS KLEINDIENST, *Left Bank Books, St. Louis, MO*
FRANK KRAMER, *Harvard Bookstore, Cambridge, MA*
RUPERT LECRAW, *Oxford Books, Atlanta, GA*
TERRI MERZ AND ROBIN DIENER, *Chapters,*
 Washington, DC
MICHAEL POWELL, *Powell's Bookstore, Portland, OR*
DONALD PRETARI, *Black Oak Books, Berkeley, CA*
JACQUES RIEUX, *Stone Lion Bookstore, Fort Collins, CO*
ANDREW ROSS, *Cody's, Berkeley, CA*
HENRY SCHWAB, *Bookhaven, New Haven, CT*
RICK SIMONSON, *Eliot Bay, Seattle, WA*
LOUISA SOLANO, *Grolier Bookshop, Cambridge, MA*
JIM TENNEY, *Olsson's Books, Washington, D.C.*
DAVID UNOWSKY, *Hungry Mind Bookstore, St. Paul, MN*
JOHN VALENTINE, *Regulator Bookshop, Durham, NC*

Available now from the Flushing office
BACK ISSUES OF THE PARIS REVIEW

No.		
18	Ernest Hemingway Interview; Giacometti Portfolio; Philip Roth.	$25.00
25	Robert Lowell Interview; Hughes Rudd, X. J. Kennedy.	10.00
30	S. J. Perelman and Evelyn Waugh Interviews; Niccolo Tucci, 22 poets.	10.00
35	William Burroughs Interview; Irvin Faust, Leonard Gardner, Ron Padgett.	10.00
37	Allen Ginsberg and Cendrars Interviews; Charles Olson, Gary Snyder.	10.00
44	Creeley and I. B. Singer Interviews; James Salter, Diane di Prima.	15.00
45	Updike Interview; Hoagland Journal; Veitch, Brautigan, Padgett, O'Hara.	10.00
46	John Dos Passos Interview; Thomas M. Disch, Ted Berrigan, Kenneth Koch.	10.00
47	Robert Graves Interview; Ed Sanders, Robert Creeley, Tom Clark.	10.00
62	James Wright Interview; Joe Brainard, Christo Portfolio.	10.00
63	J. P. Donleavy and Steinbeck Interviews; Louis Simpson, Robert Bly.	10.00
64	Kingsley Amis and P. G. Wodehouse Interviews; Diane Vreuls, Thomas M. Disch.	10.00
66	Stanley Elkin Interview; Richard Stern, W. S. Merwin.	10.00
67	Cheever and Wheelock Interviews; Maxine Kumin, Aram Saroyan.	10.00
68	William Goyen Interview; John Updike, William Stafford.	10.00
69	Kurt Vonnegut Interview; William Burroughs, Ed Sanders, John Logan.	10.00
70	William Gass Interview; Peter Handke, William S. Wilson, Galway Kinnell.	10.00
72	Richard Wilbur Interview; Joy Williams, Norman Dubie.	10.00
73	James M. Cain and Anthony Powell Interviews; Dallas Wiebe, Bart Midwood.	10.00
74	Didion, Drabble and Oates Interviews; Vincente Aleixandre Portfolio; Max Apple.	10.00
75	Gardner, Shaw Interviews; Handke Journal, Dubus, Salter, Gunn, Heaney.	10.00
76	Ignatow, Levi, Rhys Interviews; Jean Rhys Memoir Louis Simpson.	10.00
77	Stephen Spender Interview; Mark Strand, Joseph Brodsky, Philip Levine.	10.00
78	Andrei Voznesensky Interview; Voznesensky/Ginsberg Conversation; Edie Sedgwick Memoir; T. Coraghessan Boyle, Tom Disch, Odysseus Elytis.	15.00
79	25th ANNIVERSARY: R. West Interview; Paris Review Sketchbook; Hemingway, Faulkner, Southern, Gass, Carver, Dickey, Schuyler, Gellhorn/Spender/Jackson Letters.	15.00
80	Barthelme, Bishop Interviews; Reinaldo Arenas, J. D. Salinger Feature.	10.00
81	T. Williams, P. Bowles Interviews; Wiebe, Atwood, Federman Fiction; Montale Poetry.	20.00
83	J. Brodsky, S. Kunitz Interviews; Gerald Stern/B. F. Conners Prize Poetry.	15.00
84	P. Larkin, J. Merrill Interviews; T. C. Boyle, Edmund White Fiction.	15.00
85	M. Cowley, W. Maxwell Interviews; H. Brodkey, Bill Knott Poetry.	15.00
87	H. Boll, Infante Interviews; Milosz, C. K. Williams Poetry.	10.00
88	Gordimer, Carver Interviews; Hill, Nemerov Poetry; McCourt, Davis Fiction.	10.00
89	James Laughlin, May Sarton Interviews; F. Bidart Poetry, Zelda Fitzgerald Feature.	10.00
90	John Ashbery, James Laughlin Interviews; C. Wright Poetry; E. Garber Fiction.	10.00
91	J. Baldwin, E. Wiesel Interviews; Morand, R. Wilson Fiction; Clampitt Poetry.	10.00
92	M. Kundera, E. O'Brien, A. Koestler Interviews; E. L. Doctorow Fiction.	10.00
93	30th ANNIV: Roth, Ionesco, Cortazar Interviews; Rush, Boyle Fiction; Brodsky, Carver Poetry.	15.00
97	Hollander, McGuane Interviews; Dickey, Kosinski Features; Dixon Fiction, Wright Poetry.	15.00
98	L. Edel, R. Stone Interviews; R. Stone Fiction; L. Edel Feature.	10.00
99	A. Robbe-Grillet, K. Shapiro Interviews; E. Tallent Fiction, D. Hall Poetry.	10.00
100	DOUBLE 100th: Hersey, Irving Interviews; Gordimer, Munro Fiction; Merrill, Milosz Poetry.	15.00
105	Calisher, Gaddis Interviews; B. Okri Fiction; A. Zagajewski Poetry.	15.00
106	35th ANNIV: Lessing, Yourcenar Interviews; C. Smith Fiction; Logue Poetry; Styron Feature.	15.00
108	A. Hecht, E. White Interviews; C. Baxter, J. Kauffman Fiction; S. Olds Poetry.	10.00
109	Mortimer, Stoppard Interviews; Burroughs, Minot Fiction; Mathews, Simic Poetry.	10.00
111	Fowles, Fugard, Spencer Interviews; Tucci, Gurganus Fiction; Proust, Rilke Translations.	10.00
112	Kennedy, Skvorecky Interviews; Malamud, Maspéro Fiction; Perec, Pinsky Poetry.	10.00
114	Sarraute, Settle Interviews; Matthiessen, P. West Fiction; F. Wright Poetry.	10.00
115	Murdoch, Stegner Interviews; Bass Fiction; Laughlin Poetry; Merwin Feature.	10.00
116	Angelou, Vargas Llosa Interviews; Perec Fiction; Ashbery Poetry; Stein Feature.	10.00
117	Atwood, Pritchett Interviews; R. Price, Stern Fiction; Kizer, Logue Poetry.	10.00
118	Bloom, Wolfe Interviews; Tolstaya Fiction; Ashbery Poetry; Carver, Burgess Features.	10.00
119	Grass, Paz Interviews; M. McCarthy Feature; DeMarinis Fiction; Bonnefoy, Hacker Poetry.	10.00
120	Hall, Morris Interviews; Milosz Feature; Brodkey, Mailer Fiction; Corn, Lasdun Poetry.	10.00
121	Brodkey, Price Interviews; D. Hall Feature; Minot, West Fiction; Z. Herbert Poetry.	10.00
122	Amichai, Simon Interviews; J. Merrill Feature; Konrád, Montale, Zarin Poetry.	10.00
123	Mahfouz Interview; J. Scott Fiction; Ashbery, Sarton Poetry; Schwartz-Laughlin Letters.	10.00
124	Calvino, Paley Interviews; Grass, Johnson, Moore Fiction; Clampitt, Herbert Poetry.	10.00
125	Guare, Simon Interviews; Bass, Lopez Fiction; Hollander, Mazur Poetry.	10.00
126	Clampitt, Helprin Interviews; J. Williams, Eco Fiction; Goldbarth, Zarin Poetry.	10.00
127	Logue, Salter Interviews; Carroll, Shepard Fiction; Ammons, Swenson Poetry.	10.00
128	40th ANNIV: DeLillo, Morrison Interviews; Canin, García Márquez Fiction; Graham, Merwin Poetry; Cheever, Hemingway, Pound Documents.	15.00
129	Stafford Interview; J. Scott Fiction; Yenser Poetry; Salter, Trilling Features	10.00
130	Kesey, Snodgrass Interviews; Braverman, Power Fiction; Paz Poetry	10.00
131	Bonnefoy, Munro Interviews; Moody, Pritchard Fiction; Hacker, Merrill Poetry; Bishop-Swenson Letters.	10.00
132	Auchincloss, Gottlieb Interviews; Gass, Thon, West Fiction; Kinnell, Tomlinson Poetry; Kazin Feature.	10.00
133	Achebe, Milosz Interviews; Byatt, D'Ambrosio Fiction; Hirsch, Wagoner Poetry.	10.00
134	Hughes, Levi Interviews; Fischer, Schulman Fiction; Ammons, Kizer Poetry; Welty Feature.	10.00
135	Gunn, P.D. James, O'Brian Interviews; DeMarinis, Mayo, Prose Fiction; Rich, Wright Poetry	10.00
136	Humor: Allen, Keillor, Trillin interviews; Barth, Boyle Fiction; Clifton, Updike Poetry; Bloom Feature.	30.00
137	Sontag, Steiner Interviews; Bass Fiction; Seshadri Poem; Russian Feature.	10.00
138	Screenwriting: Dunne, Price, Wilder Interviews; Díaz Fiction; Hecht Poetry; Southern Feature.	10.00
139	Ammons, Buckley, Cela Interviews; Davenport, Franzen Fiction; Kizer Poetry.	10.00
140	Ford, Oz Interviews; Butler, Eakins Fiction; Bidart, Olds Poetry; Cooper Feature.	10.00
141	Snyder, Vendler Interviews; New Fiction; New Poetry; Marquez Feature.	10.00
142	Theater: Mamet, Shepard, Wasserstein Interviews; McDonagh play.	10.00

Please add $3.00 for postage and handling for up to 2 issues; $4.75 for 3 to 5. Payment should accompany order. For orders outside the U.S. please double the shipping costs. Payments must be in U.S. currency. Prices and availability subject to change. Address orders to: 45-39 171 Place, Flushing, N.Y. 11358
MASTERCARD/VISA # _____ EXP. DATE _____

CHICAGO REVIEW
~ Poets in Recent Issues ~

Mark Halliday	August Kleinzahler
Mekeel McBride	Nathaniel Mackey
Ralph J. Mills, Jr.	Will Alexander
Christian Bök	Benjamin Friedlander
Pam Rehm	Ronald Johnson
Fanny Howe	William Bronk
Peter Gizzi	Paul Hoover
Elizabeth Alexander	Michael Anania
Susan Hahn	Ray DiPalma
Norma Cole	John Taggart
Anne Carson	Lyn Hejinian
Carl Rakosi	Medbh McGuckian
Phillip Foss	Robert Bly
Barbara Guest	Hilda Morley
Ron Padgett	Ted Pearson
Pamela Lu	Larry Price
Alice Notley	Michael Palmer

Forthcoming:
43:3 ~ Peter Riley, Emmanuel Hocquard, Simon Cutts, Kathleen Fraser, Peter Russell
43:4 ~ Special Issue on Contemporary Poetry

One-year subscription for $18.
Save $6 off the cover price.

Foreign subscribers add $5 for postage. Institutional subscriptions are $35. Four issues per year. Make checks payable to:
CHICAGO REVIEW • 5801 S. Kenwood Ave. • Chicago IL 60637-1794
ph/fax (773) 702-0887 • chicago_review@uchicago.edu